the underdogs: a season to remember

by: lazarus lake

the underdogs: a season to remember

Available for purchase at:
www.amazon.com

ISBN:978-1727442458

The cover photo was taken by Chris Siers

How to contact the author:

lazarus lake

drystoneman@hotmail.com

dedicated to the underdogs:

alex
blake
jesse
will
grant
james
mark
grant
austin
brandon
dacota
jacob
lane
tyler
hayden
hunter
lane
seth
thomas
bryson

with a special thanks to coach mike

prologue

everything was on a path of convergence.
the time,
our lead,
and their foul trouble.

it is hard to describe the feeling of a game like this one.
your senses are so heightened that you can taste the air.
but you cannot hear the crowd.
you can feel the emotion.
you know the noise is there (in the back of your mind)
but your whole head is filled with a thousand thoughts at once.
all crystal clear.
i wonder how much adrenaline i pump through my system during a
game like this.

i know that everything met at the same time.
with the clock draining away,
they scored to cut the lead to two.
we made a huge mistake,
and a guy who should have been flying downcourt stopped and
took the inbounds pass.
right under our goal.
a preachers mill player immediately stole it,
and banked in the tying shot.
as the ball dropped thru the basket,
i could see the clock thru the glass of the backboard.
the time was clicking from 6.0 seconds to 5.9....

every season is special.
every team has its own stories.

it begins with spring practices,
and summer team camps.
every year opens with hopes and dreams
and the pursuit of a state championship.

it is the same at every school,

in every state.
until the games begin, everyone is 0-0.
and after every game
they set the scoreboards back to zero.
no matter what is expected,
every day of every season is what the team makes it
and for every team, save one,
the season ends with tears.

but the memories last a lifetime.

these are the stories of one team, and one season.

while these stories are told from my vantage point,
i am only a bit player;
an assistant coach.
these stories belong to the young men who made them happen

coach laz

underdogs

after the wear and tear of cross country season,
i took a few days off.
basketball started the next day,
but i just wasn't quite ready.

i have reached the point where i have to think about each new
season.
it has been a long run,
and even tho i still love the practices and the competition.
and still relish the challenge.
i know it cannot last forever.

i know that every season is not all fun.
a lot of it is hard.
i find myself wondering if one day i won't feel the fire anymore.
will i tire of teaching the same skills
the same lessons of sports, that are thinly veiled lessons of life.
will we tip off the ball,
and i won't have that total focus and concentration.
will victory lose its thrill
and defeat its pain.

a lot of the kids on the team i remember as babies.
some of their parents played for me.
i feel like my days in coaching are numbered.
but i knew i would be in for at least one more year.

this is the 6th season since i retired from doing the 6th grade team.
this year's senior class is the last of my 6th grade teams.
these guys have been with us for 7 and 8 years.
it would feel like quitting on them to not finish up their careers.
this is a special group of seniors.
a team that had a chance to go a long way.
i remember them as 6th graders.
we knew they were special then,
and i made a schedule to help them reach their potential.

we loaded up with bigger schools and powerhouse opponents.
and they faltered.
before christmas we struggled to win half our games.
the last game of the first season (before christmas)
we played a big, powerful team in a christmas tournament.
we held our own thru halftime,
and then the guys just gave up.
we got hammered.
the other team literally ran us off the floor.

afterwards the parents were angry,
feeling that i had set their kids up to fail.
i wasn't sure if i would still have a team after christmas.
looking at the remaining schedule,
i wasn't sure i wanted to have one.
all i could see ahead was a series of crushing defeats.

they did not lose another game.
i'm not sure what happened.
but we cut a swath thru that killer schedule,
like sherman marching thru georgia.

it was this team that amy and friend came to see play.
it was our biggest opponent
(not the best, but physically the biggest)
every kid on that team was at least a head taller than our
corresponding player.
afterwards amy's friend said;
"when your team came out, i felt sorry for you. your players were
so small....

then you beat the stuffing out of that other team from start to
finish."

last year was supposed to be our year.
we had a good record thru the first season.
the second season (after christmas) we dominated.
we went into the third season (the tournaments) on a roll.
expectations were sky high.

and, for the first time in all these years,
we went one and done.
one bad game at tournament time, and it was all over.

we have almost the whole team back this year.
but, in a cruel trick of fate, we have been bumped to double-A.
We are the smallest school in all of AA,
and we are stuck in the strongest AA district in the state.
every school is at least twice our size.
several of them are traditional state powers,
including the 2-time defending state champions.
when the pre-season picks came out, we were picked to finish last.
we are not supposed to win a single game in our district.

when i returned to practice, it did not look good.
after being so dominating in single A last season
(if you disregard our tournament failure)
it was as if the kids thought this year would automatically be the
same.
they did not seem to grasp the new situation they were in.
practices were lackadaisical and sloppy.
we had no intensity.
no purpose.
we were preparing for a tail-whipping.
our own.

i was surprised at coach mike's plan for the year.
given the tremendous physical disparity we would be facing,
i figured we would be looking to slow games down,
and try to win 30 point contests.

instead, he wanted to run.
he figured we would have trouble scoring against the much bigger
teams we would be playing,
and we'd have trouble holding onto the ball against their pressure.
he wanted to get the ball upcourt before the other defense could set
up,
and try to score on a broken floor.

i argued against it.
i've won a lot of games against superior talent,
by playing deliberate on offense
and hardnose on defense.
That is the formula everyone has always used.
coach mike is a good head coach.
he listens to his assistants.
then he makes his decision…

he was set on running.

i try to be a good assistant.
i argue my position.
then i do my dead level best to make what the head coach decides
work.
since none of us have coached a real running team,
i adopted the running game as a personal responsibility,
and set about learning what we needed to do to make it work.

around here, the popular idea of a running team is one that:
"pushes the ball up the court"
by which they mean to dribble the ball as fast as possible.

that is not a running game.
i pushed for drills where we worked on a real running game.
on every rebound or steal,
after every made basket (by the opponent)
we want to fly down the floor in our fast break lanes.
no hesitation.
no one has an assigned lane, there is no time for that.
everyone grabs the nearest lane, and flies downcourt.

our object is to get the ball down the floor with no dribbles at all.
pure passing.

after we got to where we could run the drills,
we put a watch on it.
off a rebound, we could have the ball at the opponent's basket in

3.5 seconds.
after a made basket, from the time the ball came thru the net,
we could be shooting a layup on the other end in 4.5 seconds...

every dribble added a second to that time.

from running pure drills to implementing it in play was a different
story.
and, as we approached our first game, i had no warm feelings.
i could see that the running game could work.
i had no delusion that we were ready to effectively engage it in a
game.

i had no good feeling about our first game.
the players did.
they were almost cocky.
we were opening up against a very good single A opponent.
we didn't need to load up with games against higher class
opponents.
we would face that in our regular district games.
we needed some games where we could physically match up.
our players seemed to think that labelling us as AA magically
made us bigger and stronger.
we have pretty decent talent for a single A team.
we are well below average for AA.

we played, like all teams do, just like we practiced.
we were careless, and lackadaisical.
we didn't box out, we played sloppy defense, and we took bad
shots.
our opponent jumped on us from the opening tip,
and the game got out of hand quickly.

we had a brief bright spot in the second quarter,
when we got our running game going for a few possessions.
we cut the lead to 14,
but that was as close as we would come to making a run at them.
we soon reverted to form, and the massacre continued unabated.

when both teams sent in the jv's our deficit was in the 30's.
our first experience as an AA team was a humiliating defeat.
looking around in the locker room after the game,
it was hard to read the players.
it was a pretty grim place.

sports are just like life, tho.
it isn't what happens.
it is how you respond.
the scoreboard would be back at 0-0 the next time we stepped on
the court,
just the same as it would have been had we won by 30.
we had a lot of work to do,
and now everyone knew it.

5 seconds

the day after our crushing defeat, coach mike had a funeral to
attend.
the team wasn't going to do anything except watch the game film,
and do some shooting.
since i had not had the opportunity to talk to coach mike,
i just sat back and listened.
it is important that the entire staff have the same message.
generally we see things the same way,
but i did not want to act on assumptions.

besides, listening can be good.
the kids soon forget you are there,
and you can find out what they are thinking.
the guys were not happy.
but they were not downtrodden
(at least not yet)
one kid said; "this is how it is going to be all year."
he was quickly silenced...

it was not one of the guys who would be playing a lot.

they saw their mistakes.
they saw the brief stretch where we ran effectively.
they shut off the film at the half,
and went to shoot.
they had seen enough,
they wanted to get to work.

practices were a lot different after our opener.
we went about our work with intensity and purpose.
we showed that sense of urgency that a good team has to have.
no matter what you have accomplished in sports,
tomorrow the score will still start out zero to zero.
and your opponent will want to beat you.

our next couple of games got cancelled

due to forecast ice storms that never showed.
so we went into our playday tournament game still 0-1.
we put the extra time to good use,
with quality practices.
the coaches and the kids had both been learning about this running
thing.
i wasn't sure we were ready to torch somebody.
but this time i felt like we were ready to do some damage with it.

the next opponent on our schedule was a larger school,
but not an overwhelming team.
we felt pretty good going into the game.
but a funny thing happened the day before our game.
the tournament host decided to swap opponents with us.
at the last minute, we found ourselves preparing to play preachers
mill.
preachers mill was a lot like us, they were one of the smaller
schools in their class.
unlike us, they were playing in AAA.

we were unable to find out anything about them,
except they had not lost yet.
they managed to lay hands on the tape of our first game.
i figured that was a negative for them.
no one who saw that tape would be able to take us seriously as an
opponent.
that was not the team we intended to bring
(altho the players looked identical to the naked eye)

after watching the tournament host lay waste to our erstwhile
opponent,
we got a look at our new foe during warmups.
it was not encouraging.
it wasn't that they were so much bigger than us,
it was the number of athletes.
that is one of the biggest differences between large and small
schools.
we don't go very deep before we get to kids who are not physically
ready to play high school ball;

especially against much larger and more physically mature kids.

i watched the warmups intently.
whenever i scout an opponent, i like to watch the warmups.
they tell you a lot.
they tell you if the opponent has good fundamentals,
how disciplined they are.
the warmups reveal who are the team leaders,
who are the shooters, and who are the power players.
this team was very disciplined.
the warmups were organized, and the players all fundamentally
sound.
this looked like a lot better team than the one that had massacred
us.
we were going to have our work cut out for us.
our ace in the hole was that they had seen that first game.

the game of basketball has a pace and a cadence.
there are times you go full out,
and there are times you relax.
one of the keys to the running game is to disrupt that cadence.
a true running team never lets you relax

we delivered a sucker punch right out of the blocks.
our goal in running is snowbirds.
a snowbird, for the uninitiated, is an uncontested layup
scored against an empty floor, before the defense can get back.

they scored.
we answered with a snowbird before their players got back to
midcourt.
they missed a shot,
we were laying in a snowbird before they could find the ball.
we jumped into a lead before they could figure out what hit them.
the first time out was called by preachers mill,
the coach wanted to increase their emphasis on getting back.

preachers mill was a disciplined team, and they shored up the
defense.

our torrent of freebies dried up.
the rest of the half was just exchanges of body punches.
we played them even in the halfcourt game,
and held on to that early lead.
i kept exhorting our players to keep running,
whether we were getting easy baskets or not.
keep the pressure up.
make them respond to what we were doing,
instead of the other way around.

at the half, we went over it again.
no matter how many times they got back,
keep running.
keep looking for the pass downcourt.
even the most disciplined team will have lapses when they get
tired.
they will revert to the normal cadence of a basketball game.
the way it has been played all their life.

we came out on the floor,
and the guys were taking a few shots before the start of the third
quarter.
i was sitting on the bench, watching,
and something came over me.
maybe it was a premonition.
i went out on the floor and called over a couple of our starters, will
and jesse.
"keep looking for the chance to run. no matter how often they get
back.
especially late.
they are going to make a mistake late in the game...

and it is going to be important."

like any underdog, we had to weather a storm coming out of the
locker room at the half.
we weathered it.
and then we answered.
the preachers mill team were under no delusions now.

they knew they were in a game.
screw the film.
these guys can play.

and when the post-halftime surge had crested,
and preachers mill tried to catch their breath,
we came back with another flurry of snowbirds.
the next thing i knew, we were into the 4th quarter,
and leading by 10.

preachers mill was not going down easy.
they had the physical advantage,
and they turned it on.
they launched into a full-court press.

once we master this running thing, we will love to be pressed.
presses have a fatal weakness,
they keep too many players on the wrong side of halfcourt.
if we can strike fast enough to get the ball behind the defense,
the press is dead meat.
and everything we are learning is how to strike fast.

unfortunately, one of the disadvantages of being a small school
is that we do not have the athletes to simulate a real press.
some of the finer points we have to learn during live games.

so i watched the clock with one eye,
and the game with the other.
i had to admire preachers mill.
they were a well-coached team, with a lot of heart.
they were mugging us.
we also cannot simulate the physicality that bigger teams can
unleash.
we have to learn just how strong you must be with the ball the hard
way.
i don't mean "mugging" as a bad thing.
they were doing what we would do if the situation were reversed.
and they were paying a double toll.
ramping up to that level to erase a lead is physically and mentally

13

exhausting.
and they were paying a heavy toll in fouls.

everything was on a path of convergence.
the time,
our lead,
and their foul trouble.

it is hard to describe the feeling of a game like this one.
your senses are so heightened that you can taste the air.
but you cannot hear the crowd.
you can feel the emotion.
you know the noise is there (in the back of your mind)
but your whole head is filled with a thousand thoughts at once.
all crystal clear.
i wonder how much adrenaline i pump through my system during a
game like this.

i know that everything met at the same time.
with the clock draining away,
they scored to cut the lead to two.
we made a huge mistake,
and a guy who should have been flying downcourt stopped and
took the inbounds pass.
right under our goal.
a preachers mill player immediately stole it,
and banked in the tying shot.
as the ball dropped thru the basket,
i could see the clock thru the glass of the backboard.
the time was clicking from 6.0 seconds to 5.9....

between 5.9 seconds and 5.0 seconds i thought about the overtime
situation.
they had 3 starters with 4 fouls.
they had expended tremendous physical effort in catching up.
our chances in overtime were pretty good.
i also saw coach mike jumping to call time out.
that is what you do in a halfcourt basketball game.
you want to set up your last play.

i realized that the crowd noise, that i could feel, but not hear,
was so loud that the official could not hear him.
because the official was looking the other way.
regulation time was not quite over
and we were not quite through.
4.5 seconds.
it is important.
from the time the ball passes thru the net on a made shot,
we can be shooting a layup at the other end in 4.5 seconds.
we had 5.
i remembered the countless drills.
over and over we had told our guys,
"always look to attack after a made basket. that is when people
relax...

especially after a big basket, late in the game.
when they may take just one second too long, to celebrate."

it is amazing how much you can think in 9 tenths of a second.

at 5.0 seconds will had the inbounds pass.
without hesitation, he turned and fired a pass the length of the
floor.
as i followed the flight of the ball,
i took in the whole tableau of the court.

our inbounder was standing and watching.
he should have been running,
but there was not time for a putback, anyway.
still, i made note to remind him at practice.

two of their players were still near the goal,
their arms, upraised in celebration, seemed frozen as they watched,
helplessly.
another was near midcourt on our side.
sam was nearby, not running his lane as fast as he should have
gone.
i made another note to correct that in practice.

the only man they had past midcourt was pursuing alex on the far
side,
alex was running his lane like a maniac (as he was supposed to do)
their other player was also near midcourt,
and i could see the panic, as he tried to recover.
because he had lost the man in his lane.
he had celebrated one second too long.

as the ball went on, i could not see the player attacking the basket.
the official that did not hear the timeout call
(and i noticed that coach mike had put his hands down the moment
will made his pass)
was following the play and blocking my view.
but i knew it was jesse.
it was his lane.
jesse runs the floor as well as anyone we have.

the ball disappeared behind the official
and then i saw it come up, and bank softly off the backboard,
as the clock rolled past 0.5
the final horn sounded as the ball nestled into the net, not even
touching the rim.
but i only barely heard it.
because, as the official signaled the basket good,
i could suddenly hear.
it was absolute pandemonium in the gym,
as the orange faithful went berserk.

their players looked stunned as we went thru the handshake line.
this bunch of runts,
with maybe 2 or 3 players who could even make their team;
had beaten them.

the coach had a haunted expression.

just like us,
he was probably already planning his overtime strategy at 5.0
seconds.
i knew this would be a loss that stayed with him a long time.

4.5 excruciating seconds would keep him awake tonight.
it was a very different locker room after this game, than it was the last.
as we discussed the game, will piped in;
"coach laz called it at the half. he told us they would make a mistake late; and it would be important!"

later on, when it was just me and coach mike, he told me,
"you know. we might as well end the season now.
we have already played the worst game we can possibly play.
and we have already played the best game we can possibly play.
what else is there?"

then we laughed, and headed home.
because the scoreboards already have been set back to zeros.
and tomorrow will only be what we make it.

***they are not that fast...

a few years ago one of the schools in our old district hired a former college player
to be their new basketball coach.
we read the newspaper article on his hiring with great interest.
in it, he described the type of game he liked to play,
and stated that he would be looking for kids who could play that type of game.

this was tremendously amusing to the old-timers.
because, in single A ball,
you are looking for anyone who can play basketball,
and praying that you will find 5 players who can play any type of game.
then you try to adapt what you do to fit the personnel you have.

the new coach went on to become a very good coach.
he had enough success to open up an opportunity to leave for a bigger school;
maybe one where he can find the players to play the game he wants to play.

he never found them at his single A school.
he did what we all do.
he trawled the halls for anyone who could play,
and adapted his game to the people he had.

for me, i never want to go to that big school,
where you pick and choose among talented athletes
(and feel bad for the ones you do not have room for)
i get to coach kids who i'd never be able to take at a bigger school,
and see the unlikeliest talents come forward.
i like to know that every kid has a chance to make himself a place on the team here.

how it was that coach mike decided this team should run,
i will never really understand.

we are not fast and athletic.
we do have a high basketball IQ.
and we were going to be hopelessly outmanned.
we had to do something,
or we were going to take a beating every night.

i will be honest.
i argued against it.
a good basketball staff is just like the management of any
organization.
the head man lets his subordinates express their opinion.
he listens, takes their ideas into account...

and then decides what he believes to be the best decision.
a good assistant coach makes a credible argument.
then, when the decision is made, he does his dead level best to
make it work.

and so it was
the biggest opponent of the running game
ended up taking the lead in developing it.

i am glad coach mike chose the path he chose.
this new thing is exciting and fun.
and i am learning new nuances every day.

our next 3 games were against our old rivals from single A.
we have no need to schedule up for so many out of district games
as we usually do.
because every district game will be playing up.
we have been playing our neighboring small towns since the first
high schools were built.
we were not about to throw those longstanding relationships and
rivalries away.

after the preachers mill game,
our running attack was no secret any more.
there are no secrets in high school sports.
as soon as you show something, everyone knows about it.

once it is on film,
every opponent will be studying it,
and trying to figure out how to beat it.
when someone figures out how to stop you,
everyone will know how to stop you.
then you have to come up with an answer.
every season is a chess match.
each move will be responded to with a countermove.

we had passed the hurdle of having the kids all in.
after the preachers mill game there would be no turning back.
now it was a matter of preparing for the counters.
you don't just work on your own attack,
you have to constantly be self-scouting.
"what is the weakness?"
"how would i stop this?"

but our opponents had the same problem we have.
they do not have enough athletes to simulate what we were
doing during practice.
they prepared the best they could,
but we were getting better every game.
and we were fortunate enough to be prepared for their
countermoves.
the orange blitzkrieg rained death from the sky
and snowbirds came in blizzards.
we left a path of destruction in our wake.
and we knew in our hearts,
that every opponent would be tougher the second time around.

after every blowout win,
our fan base grew.

the next opponent, mayfield, was a different story.
coach mike calls them a "renegade team."
they are a private school, and not a part of the state association.
they play in their own league.
as such, they have no eligibility rules.
even if you scout them during the season,

that is no guarantee you will scout the same players that show up
when you play.

on the other hand,
they have no network of common opponents to share information.
they came in as blind to us, as we were to them.

game night was pretty intense.
we watched their polished and talented girls team calmly slaughter
our girls.
their boys team was a little scary in their game-night clothes.
they were big.

they looked just as imposing in their uniforms, warming up.
during their layup drill,
player after player soared over the basket,
and then dropped the ball in.
(it is a technical foul to dunk during warmups)
they had players who could "play above the rim."

we have several guys who can touch the rim.
(we have a dunk play, just in case we get a player-some future
year-who can dunk)

in case you haven't guessed already,
i pride myself on my ability to scout warmups.
their warmup routine was designed to intimidate.
i found nuggets of encouragement.
fundamentals are key to basketball.
75% of our practice time is spent drilling fundamentals.
we go over and over the same basic skills,
me and coach mike constantly picking at every minute error in
technique.
our guys had been thru this routine for 7 and 8 years.

by the constant repetition,
the performance of basic skills had been moved from the brain's
outer cortex
to the basal ganglia.

there, the basic fundamentals of the game can be performed
automatically.
without thinking, without being subject to stress or emotion.

their players had also repeated their skills a million times,
until they could perform them without thinking.
but there was a difference.
their coach had not had the luxury of controlling every practice
since they were in elementary school.
correct fundamentals do not come naturally
to a certain extent, kids must be forced to do things right.
they must be drilled and drilled in doing things right.
good habits require a million repetitions.
bad habits will stick after one.

watching them warm up, i began compiling a list.
i was looking for the flaws in each player's game.
sometimes, in basketball; often for us,
you cannot simply totally stop another player.
sometimes all you can do is steer him toward what you want him
to do.

a good example was mayfield's point guard.
we had heard about him, and he was as good as advertised.
he could shoot the lights out.
he was probably within range when he got off the bus.
he was quick as lightning, and handled the ball like it was part of
his arm.
we had to contest his outside shot or he would butcher us.
but we had no player who could get close enough to contest his
shot,
and still be able to stop him from putting the ball on the floor
and blowing by them.

but he had a flaw.
the commonest flaw in self-taught players.
he could not score with his left hand.
he revealed his weakness in warm-ups,
going thru all sorts of convoluted maneuvers

22

in order to shoot inside from the left side, with his right hand.

bad technique is bad technique for a reason.
he could hit those shots in warmups.
but they are infinitely harder under duress, during play.
and those faux skills always fail you late in the game, when it counts.
we instructed the people who would be guarding him to close him out hard,
then simply keep him going left.
don't risk fouling him,
just force him to go left.
and keep him going left.

that, too, is a skill.
the instinct of a player is to foil anything the opponent wants to do.
every one-handed player's best move is to fake off hand,
then, when his opponent leaps to stop him,
reverse and go the way he wanted to go all along.
it takes practice to learn how to fill in behind,
and keep the guy going the wrong way.

player by player,
we worked out a plan for how to play each of their guys.
i felt pretty good about our chances.
i thought we could frustrate their players as the game went along.
and we had a secret weapon.
we were going to rain death on them from the sky.

i knew that someone on the other bench was doing the same thing.
and as a "renegade team" they had a lot of experience scouting warmups.
i also knew what they saw.
we had some good shooters,
and we were fundamentally very sound.
but we were so small, and so slow.
they had to be anticipating another slaughter, just like the girl's game.

in the early going it looked pretty tough.
we were playing almost entirely on defense.
we could take away most of the shots they wanted.
but it takes a lot of discipline to keep running an offense for long
stretches.
if we could keep them contained long enough,
they would take the shot we wanted them to take.
the problem was, they crashed the boards like gangbusters.
their warmup scouting told them one stopper getting back would
be plenty.
we were doing a good job boxing out,
but they were able to play over our heads,
and they were getting a lot of offensive rebounds and putbacks.
they took an early lead.

but here was where i learned something important about our
running attack.
there is a psychological component.
no good coach can stand to have his team beaten down the floor.
especially a coach who prides himself on having a team that can
run
and these guys were greyhounds.
when we got a defensive rebound,
we were scoring a snowbird in seconds.
half the time we were doing the same thing when they scored.
that is why we were playing all defense.
we were scoring almost immediately.

they called a timeout early in the 1st quarter to make adjustments.
we had already seen those counters,
we adjusted without hesitation,
and the aerial assault continued unabated.

he called a second timeout,
and their offensive rebounding dried up.
so powerful was the desire to stop our running attack,
he had given up his most effective weapon.
they were no longer crashing the boards,
everyone was getting back.

and still, we kept getting behind the defense.
soon we were in the lead.
and the lead kept growing.

at the half we had few adjustments to make.
our opponent was rattled, and had, as yet, found no answers.
their coach's voice echoed thru the wall between the locker rooms.
"THOSE GUYS ARE NOT THAT FAST. AND THEY ARE
BEATING YOU DOWN THE FLOOR EVERY TIME!!!!"

was it wrong that i had to stifle a smile?

they tried everything in the second half.
they put on a full court press.
have i mentioned that we love to be pressed?
it only made things worse.
they committed frustration fouls.
that just got them in foul trouble,
to go with their other problems.
they used more timeouts.
if they could get back in the game,
they would have no timeouts for strategic use at the end.

the star point guard tried to take them on his shoulders,
hitting improbable shots from ridiculous distances.
and when we extended the defense to stop him,
he penetrated the lane again, and again.
we forced him left repeatedly,
and one twisting, contorted, wrong-handed layup after another
rolled harmlessly off the rim.
i counted a stretch of 10 attempts,
where he hit a total of 2 shots.
20% shooting will not win basketball games.

we got all the rebounds;
their players were racing down the floor to try and stop the hell
raining down from above.
and still we kept getting behind the defense.

your offense is on your own end of the floor in the second half.
and eventually i noticed that,
after every snowbird,
their players were looking over at the bench.
i followed their eyes...

their coach was standing there with his arms crossed in front of
him,
staring back at them.
his jaw set.
seething.
he looked like he might erupt at any moment.

i think he was glad to answer with his own bench,
when we sent in our jayvees halfway thru the 4th quarter.

i am getting used to seeing the shell-shocked expressions in the
handshake line.
halfway thru the first season, and we are 5-1.
our players are confident and happy.
our fans think we are invincible.
the team that drubbed us in game 1 is still undefeated,
and we are still the only team to have beaten preachers mill.
but the coaches know, our toughest opponents are still ahead.
we are still the little band of slow, unathletic guys predicted to go
winless in our district.
we get to enjoy the game all the way home.

then we have to put our minds to productive purposes.
"how would i beat us?"
"where are we vulnerable?"
it is a long season,
and all we know for sure is that we will win at least 5 games.

welcome to AA

after our guys' latest giant killing, we played college grove,
another of our old 1-A rivals.
in a foretaste of things to come,
the snowbirds were an endangered species.
there is plenty of film out there, now.
and we weren't about to sneak up on anyone else...

but we are no one-trick pony.
we have a pretty fair halfcourt game.
it was a comfortable, if not overwhelming, win.

the next game was the one i had been dreading.
our first district opponent was elkton.
elkton has been an AA power for decades.
coach billy has been there for over 30 years
(god help me; i remember him as a player!)
he has forgotten more basketball than i will ever know.

i have heard people say he is not a great coach,
he just has great players.
it is true that elkton has had a history of phenomenal talent.
but if you can't coach, talent is not enough.
his teams do play an up-tempo game.
they press, and run.
when you have the athletes,
you want to play an athletic game.

we had played elkton in a tournament about 10 years ago.
we had one of our good teams (won our district that year)
they had the number one prospect in the state.
we stayed with them for a half,
and considered that a signal achievement.

coach mike had scouted their game on tuesday.
his report was grim.
he kept saying;

"they are so FAST. they aren't just quick, they are FAST...
i just don't know if we can keep up."
there were no weak points to target with our game plan.
we would just have to play the game possession by possession.

on the way down
(and the trip to elkton is a loooong drive)
sandra asked how we would do.
i told her i knew we would lose.
i just hoped we could keep it respectable.
she was mad at me;
"why are you even going, if you aren't going to try?"
she might not ever fully understand.
"oh, we are going to try to win. but you have to be realistic."

i was surprised how many fans we brought.
but our previous giant killings, blowout victories, and winning
streak had made us a lot of friends.
we filled one half of the lower level of one side of the gym....
thankfully, the quadrant behind our bench.
but our fans got pretty subdued when warmups started.
our guys looked like they had wandered into the wrong gym.
our fans thought they had seen big teams before.
this was a big team.
they would probably be the best legitimate high school team we
would play all season.
to make matters worse, blake, our biggest player and best athlete
had torn ligaments in his ankle in practice.
he was on the bench with crutches.
the roster of guys we could afford to put on the floor was pitifully
small.
i filled out my sheet to track the minutes played
(so we could rest people)
and then laughed.
i showed it to coach mike, and said;
"not much use in tracking minutes tonight."
he laughed back.
"nope. tonight they are just going to have to tough it out."

the game started like it would confirm my worst fears.
we could not even get a shot off.
the parameters of every sport change, as you advance to different levels.
we were now, officially, playing at a different level.
gaps that we were used to being big enough to pass thru
were not sufficient.
it was like our opponent was playing on a smaller floor.
to make matters worse,
most of our players simply could not afford to get caught in a one on one situation.
they would simply take the ball away from us.
our offense had to take on a "keep away" look.
we had to keep the ball moving, and away from the defensive pressure.

on the bright side, our team defense was playing magnificently.
coach mike was on top of his game,
and we employed an ever changing array of zones to keep elkton off balance.
they were disciplined and well-coached
and they moved the ball around for long periods of time,
trying to diagnose our defense,
and find the weak spots.
our guys played inspired, scrambling about to plug gaps
and cover shifts...

even the most disciplined team will eventually succumb to their weakest link.
someone will get impatient and take a less than perfect shot.
and when they did, we boxed out better than we have ever boxed out before.
we were aided in getting our defensive rebounds by our reputation as a running team.
coach billy was not about to give us our most feared weapon.
even the mighty elkton respected our lightning attack
and they got back rather than crash the boards all out.

elkton was not giving us any snowbirds,

but our running attack was still paying dividends.
and, on the other side,
practicing against ourselves has made us a very good get-back
team.
we were not making it easy for them to run either.

none the less, we were down 9-0 before we finally got off a shot.
it was not a great shot.
not the kind of shot you'd want to make your living on.
but it was the best (make that only) opening we had seen.
will shot a fall-away 3-pointer, with a hand in his face....

and hit it.

i was just glad we scored.
thank god, we would not be shut out.

after that, it was all out war.
we played possession by possession.
we contested every defensive possession like our lives depended
on it.
we ran our offenses with a singular determination.
here and there, we would get an open look.
when we did, we hit the shots.
despite getting no rewards,
we kept running our lanes.
if we could not score,
at least we could make them respond to us
instead of us always trying to answer to what they were doing.

when we hit a shot, and took a 14-13 lead,
it was like a dream come true.
we actually had a lead.
it was a great victory simply to hold a lead just once.

it was short lived,
but even after we were behind,
we continued to play hard,
and we clung to them like cockleburs.

right before the half, the snowbirds finally arrived.
approaching the half, elkton relaxed just a little.
they expected us to play for the last shot on consecutive
possessions.
that is what everyone does in the last 30 seconds.
it is what we usually do.
instead we got bang-bang back to back layups.
and suddenly we were up by 3.
when their last shot skipped off the rim,
we went to the locker room,
incredibly, unbelievably, with a lead.

our crowd, which had gone from funereal to ecstatic as the half had
played out,
did something i have never seen before.
they gave us a standing ovation as we headed to the locker room.
i had to smile to myself.
they knew it couldn't possibly last.
we had to celebrate while we could.

in the locker room, i found the jv's had raced in to occupy every
available bench;
while our starters were left to stand.
i rousted them out and told our guys to rest while they could.
this game was only going to get more intense.

coach mike talked also about "weathering the storm."
they were going to come out like a house fire.
we had stung them on their home floor,
and they were about to come after us with everything they had.
there weren't many adjustments to make.
we were playing about as well as we possibly could...

correct that. we were playing better than we possibly could.

we were going to have to play better than that,
if we wanted to leave this gym with a win.

we were not disappointed with how elkton came out in the second
half.
the game went from total war for every possession,
to nuclear war.
the irresistible tide washed over us and submerged us.
but we did not flinch.
and when that surge of emotion wore off,
we came storming back.
the 3rd quarter ended with us back up by a point,
and both teams totally spent.
the only thing to do...

was to ramp play up another level.

it had now reached a point where it was not just every possession.
it was every pass and every rebound.
for us, this was a huge gym
seats on the floor,
seats behind the goal,
and a balcony.
their fans had filled up every seat our fans didn't fill,
and people were standing in the doorways.
they are used to winning.
they are contenders at the top level.
all those state tournament, and state championship banners hanging
on the walls
announce to any visitor just who the elkton are, and just where you
are playing.
somebody's crowd was roaring continuously,
the sound shifting back and forth across the gym
matching the shifting action on the floor.
there was no underdog any more.
a weiner dog was fighting a pit bull.
and the pittie had his hands full.

they threw everything they had at us.
if you ever want to scout elkton, get a film of this game.
there is nothing in their arsenal that went unused.
and our little band of giant killers simply refused to surrender the

lead.
if they scored, we found a way to answer.

we knew they had to press us eventually.
they are a pressing team.
the press is their game.
wisdom said to take away our most dangerous weapon.
but sometimes you just have to do what you have to do.

finally, they called a timeout,
and we knew what was coming....

have i ever mention that we love to be pressed?
and i mean, really, really love to be pressed.

the tally on the press?
4 snowbirds against only 2 turnovers.
in the twinkling of an eye,
we were running out the clock,
and they were forced to foul.

the game was not over by a longshot.
atypically, we did not hit but half our free throws.
(our guys had to be utterly exhausted)
and they drained one desperation three after another.
finally, they hit the three that cut the margin to one possession,
we led by only 3.
they had to foul us on the inbounds play,
because they had run out of timeouts.
(keeping track of the other team's timeouts is important)

as we walked down to shoot our free throws,
i tugged at coach mike's sleeve.
"call timeout!"
he looked a question mark at me.
i pointed to the clock;
"10.3 seconds, and they have no timeouts."
i didn't have to go into detail.
every coach understands what that means.

if we hit either free throw,
and then force them to dribble the ball up the floor,
it is impossible for them to score with more than 5 seconds left.

with no timeout for them to call,
we would not have to inbound the ball again.
if we hit one free throw, and play it out right,
we cannot lose.

coach mike called timeout.
and i felt like a good assistant coach.
game strategy is enough to utilize a head coach's every synapse
(even with the gallon of adrenaline we had probably both pumped
into our system)
my job is not to be an extra head coach,
it is to keep track of the little things.
clocks, timeouts, and fouls are among my responsibilities.

as it turned out;
they missed the shot,
we got the rebound,
and shot meaningless free throws with 3.5 seconds on the clock.

our crowd did not want to leave.
their crowd just sat, in stunned silence.
their team appeared to be in shock going thru the handshake line.
and the feeling i felt,
the feeling i know i was sharing with everyone on our team...

i cannot describe it.

on the way home i thought about all the big wins i have seen.
it has been a long run,
with more highs than i deserve,
and not near as many lows.
the swarming midgets shocking harding on their home court.
case's team wrecking a mighty college grove team's state title
aspirations back in 2000...

and so many unlikely wins by this bunch of giant killers
over the past 8 years.
these boys that i have been lucky enough to watch grow into fine
young men.

there is a reason i was rushing to get this done today.
because tonight we play belvidere.
the scoreboards will be set back to zeroes,
and we could lose as easily as we can win.

the pundits, who only see the scores,
and have never seen the teams,
have rewarded us with a lofty ranking.
we are still the only team to beat preachers mill.
we are the first team to beat elkton
(and we did it on their home floor!)
the only thing that ranking will get us,
is everyone's best game.
now, we are the team that can make someone's season.

and we are still who we are.
we are still too small.
we are still too slow.

all we have are 7 wins.
all we are guaranteed is that we will lose fewer than 20 games.
before the season, our goal was to just beat one of the bottom
teams in our district.
that would have been an upset.
we wanted to show that we belonged.

we belong.

and i can feel the adrenaline for tonight already.
winning or losing will be decided by what we do on the floor.

god, i love this game.

when you get tired, run harder

we have these running drills we do in practice.

i will respond for you;
"of course you have running drills you do in practice. you are a
running team."
but it goes deeper than that.
running drills cannot just be what we do.
they must become who we are.

the funny thing is;
we are not especially fast.
but when everyone is tired,
the man who runs hard looks fast.

in one drill we send a group of 3 men to each goal.
and add 2 outside players on the wings at the near goal.
5 men go to center court,
and come at the near goal on offense.
whether there is a score, a defensive rebound, or a turnover
the defense goes on offense at full speed.

now, i am sure,
from the bleachers,
it looks like we are just flying up and down the court willy-nilly.
but what we are running is an offense.
there are positions and assignments.
there is just no time for people to run to specific places.
everyone fills the nearest spot.
so everyone has to be able to play every position.
we have no name for the offense.
in my head, i like to call it "hell"
because what we want to bring to the floor is 32 minutes of hell.

in this particular drill,
the defense always has 3 people already back.
the teams we play know what is coming.

they are going to be running their butts off,
trying to get back.

our objective is to get there before that defense can get set.
we have a dozen different ways to get to the basket
in less than 5 seconds.
if we can beat the last 2 offensive players down the floor,
the handful of guys that are "back"
face an opponent with men coming at them from all directions.
even when they know what we want to do,
it is hard to stop.
if the defense tries to take something away,
we have automatic responses,
to attack the gap left in the defense.
5 men have to operate with one mind,
responding in split seconds.
score, turnover, or rebound,
the ball is coming back the other way in 5 or 6 seconds.

the core of the offense is to avoid dribbling at all costs,
and advance the ball with quick passes.
to do that,
everyone has to run at breakneck speed.
all the time.

this particular drill goes up and down the floor
at a ridiculous tempo.
and never stops.
it is, in effect, a brutal interval workout...

with a basketball.

and like any interval workout,
players are soon gasping for air.
10 minutes of that is harder than any quarter of basketball we will
ever play.
15 minutes of it is hell.

and when the guys start to get tired,

we tell them to run harder.
runners know how that works.
what is the best thing to do when it hurts?

run harder.

our guys can tell you these things.
because we tell them every day.
"when it hurts, run harder. if we are tired, our opponent is dying."
"take away their legs, and you take away their heart."

our guys want to hang a sign over the door to the gym that says;
"welcome to hell"
we all know we can't do that.
but we can think it.

there are a lot of variations on the offense.
ways to attack after a steal.
changes to the lanes when we get behind the defense.
there are a lot of decisions that have to be made and acted on,
in 3 to 5 seconds.
if you want to do it right,
a running basketball team has to do a lot more than just fly up and
down the court.

i grade us out at a little over 50% efficiency.
we will have to get better.....

as for the finish to the first season:

there was no letdown against belvidere.
belvidere has a young and inexperienced team.
they have been struggling to find themselves this season.

we allowed them no time to look for themselves in our gym.
(the one we call hell)
the lesson of last year's letdown,
that ended our tournament run at one game,
had not been forgotten.

we came out sharp, and aggressive.
after the games we had been thru,
belvidere seemed small and slow.

they knew what was coming,
and did a halfway decent job of getting back.
but once there, they were hit by a bewildering avalanche.
and the endless blitzkrieg assault
soon had them bent over, holding their shorts and gasping for air.
if you can't contain us,
we are not fun to play.

we were up by 20 in the first quarter.
by the half, we were deep in our bench.

the jvs played the entire 4th quarter.

our inevitable letdown came in the next game, against boones hill.
boones hill had athletes equal or better than ours.
they had a canny, experienced coach.
i have a lot of respect for coach lavon.
his teams are always well prepared, and play hard.
he always has something up his sleeve.
there are a lot of good, young coaches.
but there is no substitute for experience.
coach lavon is not inclined to just respond to you.
he will try to gain the initiative,
and make you respond to him.

it was a classic game,
with us in the unfamiliar role of the favorite,
with an opponent playing over their heads against us.
the momentum went back and forth.
the lead followed suit.
we just weren't sharp.
we dribbled way too much.
boones hill showed ways that our running game *can* be slowed
down.

we got lackadaisical on defense
and had lapses in boxing out.
boones hill made us pay for every shortcoming.

every time we got a little breathing room,
and thought we were about to take control,
boones hill came storming back.
at the end of the third quarter,
we trailed by a point.
a season is made of tests.
tests of how you respond to every situation.
we had been on the other side of this equation a lot.
an underdog, with a late lead.
8 minutes to play for a signature win.

this was our first good taste of the other side.

we responded the way good teams respond.
we found the magic one more time.
we ripped off a streak of quick baskets
and were up by 10 in the twinkling of an eye.
after that, it was only a matter of finishing.
and our guys have learned how to finish.

all that remained of the "first season" was our christmas
tournament.
watching our practices, i felt pretty good about how christmas
would go.
despite all the holiday distractions,
we were focused.
everyone was there when we practiced at 0800.
everyone was there when we practiced at 1830.
we would play college grove and park city,
among the last of our old district rivals on the schedule.
teams we matched up with well, physically.
of course, beating us now would make their first seasons.
they would take the floor hungry for a piece of us.
this is what success gets you.
everyone's best game.

and a target on your back.
what good teams have to do in games they should win,
is come out swinging and strike the first blow.
take away the opponent's legs.
take away their hope.
take away their heart.

game one, we came out with our best defensive effort of the year,
so far.
a swarming amoeba stymied every attempt to find an open shot,
or a path to the basket.
our cadre of pickpockets turned every pass or dribble into an
adventure.
and we ran like men possessed,
warming the hearts of the coaches
as we finally implemented some of the finer points of the running
game.

we blew out to a 31-7 lead by the early 2nd quarter,
and the game was effectively over.
once again our deep bench and jvs got a lot of playing time.

the next night, last night,
we came back with more of the same.
after witnessing the utter annihilation of our first opponent,
last night's opponent probably harbored some doubts from the
outset.

they found their worst fears confirmed,
facing a 33-8 deficit and our deep bench early in the second
quarter.

and so we concluded the first season (thru christmas) on a high
note.
we are 11-1, with 11 straight wins.
even sandra commented that we were not on our normal track;
"usually we have our struggles early in the season, and come on
strong after christmas."

of course, we are now starting all over with the second season.
we beat a number of bigger, more athletic teams in the first season,
but we also played a lot of games against teams our size.

the second season we will see most of our district opponents.
we can expect to be outsized, outnumbered, and out-athleted
almost every game.
there is a good reason we were picked to finish dead last.
and now, no one will be overlooking us.

we have accomplished a lot already this year.
but in sports you can never rest on your past achievements.
for all the highs,
we are not even guaranteed a winning record.
we'll be taking off tomorrow.
then it is back to work.

we have to get a lot better before we play again.
the scoreboards are set at zero to zero.
and what we do from here forward,
will determine whether we win or lose.

nice

all winning streaks have to end sometime.

i had been thinking about the recent thread on being "nice" lately.
of course, being nice in everyday life,
and being nice in the context of competition are different things.
when the game is on, there is not time to worry about being "nice."

it is not the time or place to be chatting people up,
or to sit and think about how to phrase everything you say.
even if your mind is racing a hundred miles an hour,
there isn't room in there to worry about being polite.
whether you are a player or a coach (or even an official)
you can't wear your feelings on your sleeve.

after the game is a different matter.
in my mind it is tougher to be a good winner than a good loser.
everybody comes in wanting to win.
everyone does their best to win.
losing is always the same.
you are disappointed.
all that is required is that you control your emotions.
you congratulate the winner.
you don't make excuses.
you don't show your butt.
it is not about you.
the day belongs to the winner.
if you feel like you have to say something,
you talk about how well they played, how well prepared they were,
and how good they are.
and then you go home to try to get better.

winning has a lot of faces.
sometimes you are just better than your opponent.
you can't act like you feel that way.
sometimes it is a huge upset.
no matter how big the game,

i try to have the same comportment on the bench,
and in the handshake line.
every player who played well,
i try to address them personally, by number,
to tell them they played well, or are a good player.

some wins are hugely exciting.
the improbable upset,
the championship games,
games with huge stakes.
just as we have to discipline our behavior in defeat,
we have to discipline our behavior in victory.
outside the spontaneous response when a game is won at the last
second,
celebrations are for the locker room.

i like to think that film of my actions on the bench
or in the handshake line
would not reveal whether we were winning or losing.

we came back from an abbreviated christmas break with a game
against belvidere.
it would be one of only two remaining games against schools our
size.
belvidere is a young team, in rebuilding mode,
and we had beaten them severely during the first season.

our game plan was not "nice."
we wanted to come out smoking and shatter any confidence they
might have built back up.
it was decidedly not nice how the thought made my blood course
faster.

most of the basketball team had run cross country with us in the
fall.
it had turned out to be much more demanding than they expected,
and most of them had dropped off the team as the season went on.
despite that, the work had paid dividends.
we had brought an amped up tempo to the game of basketball,

and between the cross country experience,
and a carefully managed rotation,
other teams had been wilting at the pace of our games.
by the second quarter we enjoyed seeing our opponents bent over,
holding onto their shorts
while our guys appeared unfazed.
i heard players on our team who did get fatigued admonished;
"you should have run cross country."
we have not been fun to play.

in the christmas tournament,
we played a team we had already played once.
apparently their coach didn't warn them who they would face,
because when the teams took the floor before the game,
their captain said to ours;
"oh no. not y'all again!"
that is, actually, the effect we want to have.

belvidere had a different attitude altogether.
knowing they could not run with us,
they set about controlling the tempo of the game at all costs,
running long offensive sequences looking for easy shots,
and with some new tricks to try and disrupt our pedal to the metal
offense.

they did a good job of it.
on top of that, we had an "off" night shooting.
the two teams wrestled for control of the pace;
belvidere running long, slow sequences,
and us racing down the floor like greyhounds.
the early edge went to belvidere
as they slowly pulled out to a 17-11 lead.

what we would really like to do,
is complement our high octane offense
with a flesh eating press.
unfortunately, we really aren't that fast.
and we are not exceptionally quick...

but we are in condition.
even tho they were controlling half the tempo,
we could see the effect of racing us back every time on defense
starting to wear on the belvidere players.

so we launched into all-out half-court pressure,
robbing them of their only respite.
there was a momentary loss of composure at the assault,
and, scoring in bunches, as we are so capable of doing,
we took an 18-17 lead before they could call timeout.

during this part of the game, the "nice" issue came up again.
one of our inside players got into foul trouble early.
with blake still out with his ankle injury, we are desperately thin
there.
only two of the four posts we want to rotate ran cross country.
blake and the one now in foul trouble.
the remaining two would have to have help to get thru the half at
our pace.

at full strength we run a 9 man rotation.
on the bench we have the 4 reserves at the end near the scorer's
table
we can get them in and out quickly,
we can give them instructions,
and coach mike can see who he has available.
the coaches sit in the middle
and then the rest of the players are at the far end.

with blake out, one of the seats had been left empty,
and one of the other players had taken to filling it...

who knows why.
like as not, a parent
(and parents see everything that happens,
but often do not understand why)
had told him to sit there;
"those are the only players that get sent in!"

in order to keep from exhausting our own post players
we had to send in dacota, a promising young post player to
contribute some minutes.
he is going to be a very good player for us before he is done,
but he still has a ways to go.

when we sent dacota in,
there was no empty seat at the front of the bench for the player
coming out.
bench order is one of my duties,
so, as our subbed out post came off the floor i hollered
(loudly, because the gym was loud) "G!"
as these thing so often happen,
the sound in the gym lulled, just as i yelled.
in my ears "G!" seemed to echo harshly forever.
my heart sunk, thinking i might have embarrassed the young man,
but there was no time to fix things then.
he looked at me, and i motioned with my hand for him to move
and told him;
"give jesse that seat."

i suppose that anyone in the gym who witnessed that exchange
would tell you
that i am not a "nice" person at all.
after the game, i apologized to G, telling him i did not mean for it
to sound so....
mean.
he shrugged it off;
"i understand."

he might have understood, but i bet it helped that i apologized.
the people in the bleachers, or at least his parents, might still think
i am a jerk.
but i am not there for them.
i am there for the 19 young men on our roster.

belvidere finally ran totally out of gas in the waning moments of
the half.
they had more kids calling to be taken out

than they had frontline people to send in,
and we opened up a 10 point margin with another run.

i am sure the half seemed like the fastest 10 minutes of their young
lives.
but most of the belvidere team seemed to have gathered
themselves.
their young point guard had borne the brunt of the half court
assault,
and i gleefully saw him holding his shorts during free throws,
barely a minute into the second half.
he was totally gassed.

moments later he called to come out,
and played only sparingly for the remainder of the game.
that was a blow to belvidere.

but they fought on.
they stuck with their game plan,
and scratched and clawed their way back into the game.
they would work and work to chip away at our lead,
and then we would make another spurt and open it back up.

as the game wore on,
i developed a growing admiration for this team.
clearly, they were exhausted.
but this time they did not flinch.
we were not on our best game,
but belvidere was shooting out of their minds.

as the game wore on into the final quarter,
belvidere was holding on by a thread.
after each run, we would be a little further ahead.
and each time they could not quite fight back as close as they had
been before.
and between their limited numbers and fatigue,
the fouls had begun to ride heavy.
all their vital players were in foul trouble.
at last, we made a run that opened up an 18 point lead,

with only four minutes to go.
i was sure that this time we had broken them.....

they came down and hit a 3 from downtown.
15
we bobbled a fast break pass at the basket and turned it over.
another miraculous 3.
12
we came down and got fouled (fouling out one of their starters)
we hit only the second free throw
13
as they prepared to come down with the potential to cut it to 10
coach mike commented;
"we just can't put them away."

every now and then i have something of value to say;
"sure we can. we already have...

run 20 passes"
i pointed at the clock.
"there are only 3 minutes left. even if they cut it to 10 this trip,
if we hold the ball it is over.
they are too tired to chase us, and in too much foul trouble to foul
us."

they ended up fouling us,
which sent a second starter to the bench.
but the belvidere coach had sent his JV's to the table as soon as we
started 20 passes.
he knew it was over.
we sent ours in as well,
and the game ended honorably for all involved.

after we came out of the locker room,
i looked for the belvidere coach, to congratulate him for his game
plan and his team's play.
but i didn't see him.
i did see their only senior, who had played an outstanding game.
he was walking towards me looking tired, and sort of down.

so i met him and offered him a hand to shake;
"you guys played great tonight."
his face lit up as he took my hand
"thank you."
"you had a great game plan and you executed it beautifully.
you all are on your way."
"i hope you are right."
"i am sure of it. by tournament time y'all will be hard to handle."

it seemed like he walked away standing a little taller.
defeat is temporary,
hope will carry you on to fight another day.

at this point i am sure you are wondering about the first line.
because our winning streak did not end on this night.
we extended it to 12 games.

but it will end tuesday.
tuesday is the day when i will have to work to be "nice."

by most standards i have no issue with tuesday's opponent.
their people are nice.
their players will display good sportsmanship.
but i will have to focus on being "nice."
this is a game that should never be played.

tuesday we play AHA.
they have recruited one of the best teams in the country.
yes, the country.
the entire united states.
it will be the most talented basketball team that has ever been in
our gym.
unless we have a college game someday, it will be the best team
that ever plays here.
and not just any dinky college game, at least a mid-major college
game.
they have the best team in tennessee, in any classification.
they have not lost a game in state for years.
they could beat most any of the small college teams.

why will we lose?
well, not because we don't try to win.
every coach indulges himself in the fantasy that any game might be
won.
but the belvidere game was an eye opener.
we are still what we are.
we are a really good single A team,
overachieving to be competitive with AA.
AHA's presence in AA is a joke.
and that is probably as much as i should say about it.
nothing else i have to say is "nice" at all.

but here is the way it is.
in AA, a team with a single D-1 college prospect is a contender.
a team with two would be a power.

this team will start 5.
our school had a D-1 prospect once...

back in the late 1980's.
he scored 28 points and pulled down 16 rebounds a game his
freshman year.
i only have his freshman stats,
because a private school recruited him away after that.

we have a gameplan.
we will work on it tomorrow.
(if travel is possible)
and tuesday we will play our hearts out
and no matter how well we play, we will lose.

the aftermath

just so you'll know:

halftime 20-66
3rd quarter 36-97
i don't remember the final.
but it was bad.

afterwards their coach apologized for beating us by 60.
it seems they had a player trying to set some sort of record.
how much can a record set in a "game" like that mean?

the game was,
as ALL of their AA games should be,
a farce.

there is a class for the schools that put together teams,
rather than playing with the players they have.
they should grow up and play in it.

even if it means not being guaranteed to win every game.

after the apocalypse

i was worried about how the team would respond after our last
game.
one good thing; it is basketball season.
i would not have to wait long to find out.
the other good thing; the scoreboard would be set back to zero to
zero.
there was no 60 point deficit to erase.

the guys seemed flat at practice wednesday.
thursday started out no better,
but as the session progressed,
we seemed to pick up intensity.
still, i wasn't sure what to expect.
we played elkton again.
this time at home.
shocking them at their place had been one of our biggest wins ever.
to repeat it, indeed, to win any game in our AA district,
we cannot just play well.
we have to play insane, over our heads basketball.

watching elkton' players entering the gym was hardly comforting.
they were every bit as big and intimidating looking as the last
opponent.
they weren't as deep.
and i knew they weren't as athletic.
they did have the one player who will be in the sec next year.
that is a lot more than we can claim...

and i knew for sure they would want us bad.
big brother was here to put little brother in his place.
i could see it on their faces.
there was no cutting up and jostling around like last time.
elkton was here for business.
the little runts in orange were not a joke any more.

if i thought we would have to weather the storm early,

i was sadly mistaken.
they came in planning to strike first and strike hard;
instead it was us that landed the first blow.
we jumped up 5-0 right out of the blocks.

after that, it was all out war.
elkton hit us with everything they had.
they pushed us to the limit,
but our guys simply refused to surrender the lead.

unlike the last game,
we had an opponent with weaknesses,
and coach mike's game plan was letter perfect.

we ran the floor with determination.
we did not score a lot of points from running to start with,
but we kept running.
if we managed to catch someone slacking on their assignment,
we scored.
and in a game where every point was golden,
those baskets were like the pot at the end of the rainbow.

running also served another purpose.
most teams play mainly 6 or 7 players.
with blake in his first game back, we had 9.
elkton could prevent our fast break baskets.
but to do it, they had to run...

and run...

and run some more.

our cross country guys can run all day.

besides blake, our most athletic player, being back
there was one other difference from our december game.
in december we had been shocked by the speed and athleticism.
after the apocalypse last time out,
this game was almost felt like it was in slow motion.

we had taken a severe beating,
but truly, anything that doesn't kill you, makes you stronger.
and we had not died that night.

as has been our pattern,
the last part of the first half the attrition began to take its toll.
our tiny lead extended to 10 in the last few minutes.
this time there was no standing ovation just because we were
ahead.
this game, we were playing as equals.

they started the second half with a flourish,
cutting into our margin,
but in the last part of the third, and the early 4th we asserted
ourselves.
almost without realizing it,
we extended our lead to 14 points.

but elkton is a quality team.
they have good players, and a good coach.
they have a program with pride and tradition.
with the clock running down,
they mounted one final charge.

our lead began to shrink
as the two teams fought tooth and nail,
up and down the court.
with 3 minutes to go, they hit a huge 3,
to cut the lead to 5.
got a defensive stop,
and scored again to cut it to 3.

someone asked me, after the game;
"were you sweating, when they cut it to 3?"

i was kind of surprised.
i was worried before the game,
but not at the end.
their players were exhausted.

with our long bench, and carefully managed minutes,
we were sending in fresh bodies to close out the game.
their fouls were spread over 5 people,
and the desperation final drive had them in a world of foul trouble.
we had 9 players sharing the foul load.
no one was in trouble.

but, more than that,
i have been with these players since they were in elementary
school.
if there is one thing they do better than anything else;
they win close games at the end.

the elkton tide reached its height at 3 points.
we came back and scored a couple of baskets,
and then we went to 20 passes.

it was a story we have played out before.
they were too tired to chase, and in too much foul trouble to foul.

i have to admit that i was worried how we would respond after the
apocalypse.
i should have looked back on when these guys were on my 6th
grade team.

after a pretty mediocre start to our season,
we played a much bigger and more powerful team in our last game
before christmas.
after scrapping for a half, we ran out of gas.
we took such a horrible beating in the second half that the guys just
quit,
and we got routed.
i had parents chew me out for scheduling such a game.

with the remainder of our season being against similar opponents,
i wondered if my team would even come back to play it out.

they did not lose another game that year.
that is who our guys are.

we still have a long way to go this season, and a tough row to hoe.
we will still be outmanned every time we take the court.
we will still have to play insane, over our heads basketball every
night,
if we are to have a chance.
we are not guaranteed to win a single game more than we have
now.

no matter how it comes out,
i wouldn't trade my seat on this bench,
for one with the most stacked team on earth.

island hopping

i marvel at the resiliency of this team.
unbowed in defeat,
unfazed by hostile gyms,
undaunted by the odds against them.
they can be counted on for one thing.
every night they show up to play.

a basketball season is much more than just a series of games.
it is also a 3-month game of chess.
every team must constantly reinvent itself.
if you are not succeeding,
then it is a search for that combination that allows you to win.
if you are succeeding...

then everyone is searching for the combination that will thwart
you.

there are a lot of good coaches coaching high school basketball.
it is only a matter of time before someone finds the opening.
and once one team knows, everyone knows.

snowbirds had become an endangered species over the past few
games.
and now the burden was on us.
as an undersized, out-athleted team, the running game was paying
dividends
well beyond the points it yielded.
in order to stop us from running,
our opponents had to sacrifice crashing the boards for offensive
rebounds.
the first part of the equation for winning games
is getting all your defensive rebounds.
we needed to keep our opponents respect for our running game,
to prevent them from overwhelming us rebounding.
we needed to make them respond to something we are doing.
having the initiative is also a critical component of winning.

we are not big, we are not fast, or quick.
but our guys understand the game.
we are keeping the hammer down.

the games do not begin with the opening tip.
our opponents are not the only ones studying game film,
and constructing game plans.
every game is a contest of who can impose their will on the other.
who can make the game be played to their strengths,
and against the opponent's weaknesses.

our next game was against arno.
arno is a young team.
they are playing a lot of people,
and really seemed to be trying to find their identity.
at the moment, they were occupying the spot that had been
reserved for us;
at the bottom of the standings.
i hoped this would not be the night they found themselves.

watching them warm up before the game,
as i do before every game,
looking for insights into our opponent that cannot be gleaned from
film...

how do they relate to each other.
what do they want to do,
what do they avoid.
i was struck by their size.
after so many games that we were walking into the valley of the
giants,
on film they had looked tiny.
in my mind, i thought we were going to be the bigger team.

when we lined up for the opening tip, i was disappointed.
they were every bit as big as we were.
and i was struck by the realization that this was what we looked
like to other teams.

tiny.
no wonder every win was so stunning to the teams we were
beating.

this night would be our night.
we took control early,
and never let up.
for the first time in a long time,
our deep bench saw lots of action.

another island taken.
but there was no chance to relax.
the next stop on our road tour was at farmington.
it was the big showdown.
midway thru the season, it was only us and farmington without a
district loss.
(no one counts those other people. this season is about winning the
AA part of the district)

unlike a lot of our games, we did not give away too much in size.
they were only a little bigger than us.
it was the athleticism.
quick as cats, and able to jump out of the gym,
farmington would be a tremendous challenge.

the early part of the game was all farmington.
their swarming defense played the passing lanes like riverboat
gamblers.
we were pressed to the limit, trying to keep possession,
much less finding the tiniest sliver of an opening.
this time we were the team losing patience,
and taking bad shots.

on offense, they spread us out.
their lightning quick point guard again and again exploiting the
gaps
and penetrating the heart of our defense for easy baskets or dish
passes.

the game was loosely called, and turned into a very physical contest.
it is something we have to be able to deal with.
we cannot get where we want to go, unless we can play under any conditions.
but physical games do not favor a finesse team like us.

this time it was us watching a small deficit slowly grow larger and larger.
it took a tremendous surge before the half, to pull back nearly within single digits.

halftime adjustments were fairly simple.
we had to try to push the game to the few advantages we had.
we also had to shrink our rotation.
we count on playing a lot of guys,
but we are still a single A school in size.
some of the younger players we count on were simply physically overwhelmed.
i could put my time chart away.
the guys who *could* physically match up were just going to have to play.

our reduced lineup came out swinging in the second half.
we hit farmington with everything we had,
and they gave as good as they got.
the battle raged up and down the court.
despite their swarming efforts to get back on defense,
we occasionally found the tiniest windows to slip thru our downcourt passes.
easy baskets were scarce as hens teeth for both teams.
with the help of ours, we slowly chipped away at the lead.

we got it down to single digits.
scratching and clawing for every basket we inched closer and closer.

we were within 7 to start the 4th quarter.
a minute later we had pulled within 5.

and there we stuck.
5-7-5-7...

as the clock began to dwindle, every possession took on even more
urgency.
time after time we had defensive stands where we simply had to
get a stop.
we got the stops,
but then we could not find the tiniest crack in their defense.
we fought like wild men to keep the score at 7,
but we could not get closer than 5.
frustrated by their defense,
it was us losing our patience and taking bad shots.

and when the time came that desperate measures must be taken,
no prayers were answered.
we lost the same way we have been winning.
watching our opponent bury us at the free throw line.

when we walked out of the gym, it was farmington alone at the
top.

there was no time to feel sorry for ourselves.
we had to turn right around and travel to thompson's station.
if farmington is the quickest team in the district,
thompson's station is the biggest,
led by a pair of 6-8 type post players.
no time to mourn our first loss;
we went straight into the game plan
for playing a team that was a head taller at every position.

the beauty of basketball is that every game is unique.
After the frenetic pace of the farmington game,
we locked up in a chess match with thompson's station.

we knew that any time they got the ball around the basket,
there was little we could do to prevent them from scoring...

they knew it, too.

we relied on our defensive amoeba,
facing the ball with a sea of waving arms,
and constructing a wall around their posts,
leaving only tiny gaps to fit in passes.

they responded with patience,
working the ball around,
moving, screening, cutting inside,
searching for the misstep, for the slow shift,
for any defensive mistake.

on the other end,
we faced a wall of giants.
they were tenacious, and disciplined.
the roles were reversed,
as we worked our offense in high gear,
trying to spring anyone loose for an open look.

anyone who thinks a low scoring basketball game is boring needs
their head examined.
both teams were working their tails off on both ends of the floor.
we weren't the only team with their season on the line.
tonight's winner would still be in the chase.
the loser would be out of contention.

the difference in the game was,
when we found an opening, we got one shot.
when they got the ball in close, they scored.
when we tried to pack it in even tighter,
they sent in a little shooter to torch us from outside.
by the end of the first quarter we were down by 10.

i wondered to myself if this was the end of the dream.
how many times could we ask our guys to rise above their physical
ability.
how many times could we pull off the miracle.
on the outside i showed the same emotion that i show when we are
leading by 20.

no one should ever be able to look at you on the bench and tell if
you are winning or losing.
no one should know that there is so much adrenaline flowing
that your mind is running like a racecar.

while we didn't have many advantages, we had a few.
we were able to use our whole rotation.
and in a game being played with such intensity,
having a long bench is worth its weight in gold.

as the battle raged on into the late stages of the second quarter,
we started to find some openings.
little by little we crept back into the game.
when a late score pulled us within 4 going into the locker room,
i felt really good about our position.

i wonder if people watching the game thought we made brilliant
halftime adjustments.
our game plan going in had been sound;
no one has any secrets left by the late part of january.
we focused on tightening up the few defensive lapses we had
allowed,
and we emphasized the offenses that had been most effective.
we told the guys to keep running.
we had yet to score from it,
but it was keeping them off the boards,
and it was taking a toll on their legs.

we also refreshed our memory of the couple of special plays we
had prepared just for this game.
you always want to go into games with one or two special things
things that were prepared just for that opponent.
plays that you are certain will score.
and if the right situation never happens,
you carry them home...

plays like that will only work once.
they should not be used unless they are truly needed.

both teams came out in a defensive mode.
the third quarter was total intensity,
we only scored 11 points the entire quarter...

we held them to 8.

we might have never held a lead,
but we went into the final quarter trailing by a single point.
i quickly tallied the time chart as the quarter ended.
we had worked it perfectly to our plan;
the minutes spread over 9 players.
all our key guys were fresh for the homestretch.
i showed it to coach mike, and we shared a little smile.
then i put it away.
at nut cutting time there is no more math.
we just play.

as we filtered our front line onto the floor during the early minutes
of the final quarter,
you could see the momentum swing.
after fighting just to stay alive for most of the game,
we started to take control of the action.
their offense sputtered and faltered, but their defense held strong.
with just over 3 minutes to play, trailing by 2,
we pulled out one of those special plays.

it caught thompson's station completely by surprise,
and we scored an uncontested layup.
for the first time since 0-0, we were tied.
coach mike looked at me and laughed.

we had run it who knows how many times in practice.
it had never worked.
but in practice, the defense knew what was coming.

rattled, thompson's station finally lost their offensive discipline
and took a quick shot.
we got the rebound and came down with the chance to take our
first lead of the game...

i knew what will was going to do before he did it.
i have been watching these men since they were little boys,
and i knew that look.
he was about to launch a 25 footer with a hand in his face.
just the sort of shot selection that had killed our chances against
farmington.

almost without thinking i hollered; "NO!"
not that he could have heard me.
i realized as i said it,
that for some reason the gym had been awash with the roar of the
crowd for a long time.

the most important possession of the game,
and we choose it to take our first bad shot.
i watched it arch thru the air with a sense of impending doom.
we had worked so hard.
we had defied all the odds.
the game was in our hands,
and i could feel it slipping thru our fingers like sand...

then the ball dropped cleanly thru the net.

coach holly, was staring at me intently.
she was close enough to have heard me.
i just shrugged;
"it was still a bad idea."

he did not take another.
we shot nothing else but free throws the rest of the way,
sinking every one until the game was safely locked away.
this night, it was someone else's chance to chase and foul
and fire up long shots in desperation.

our island hopping campaign is over,
that was the end of our road games
except a trip to get our second scheduled beating friday.
this time the kids all know the score.

it is a chance to play against college level talent and try to get
better.
there is no worry about any psychological hangover.

we have three district games left, and one non-district, all at home.
we are 15-2 (15-3 if you count college level opponents)
and our fate is in our own hands.
if we win out, we will be no worse than tied for the top spot in the
district.
if someone knocks off farmington,
and there are certainly teams in our district that could,
we could win outright.

no matter what happens,
it has been one helluva season for the little team picked to finish
dead last.

i don't want it to ever end.

the window

a basketball season is, in many ways, like an ultramarathon.
a sort of a multi-month ultra.
and just like in an ultra, you start out with goals.

everyone's "goal" is to win the state.
as we all know, that is not always possible.
so there are the same tier of goals that we set in ultras
the dream goal (the state)
the realistic goal,
and the fallback goal.

as a newly minted AA team,
knowing that we would be facing schools twice our size every
night out,
even our "realistic" goal seemed like something of a dream.
we were picked by the experts to finish dead last in our new
district
and not even win a single game.
our realistic goal was to beat somebody.
anybody.
that would be a pretty good achievement.
we had reached that goal.
and then some

our dream goal was to win the district...

understanding that no one in the district even counts AHA.
they could not lose a game if they tried.
what the state association is deeming "second place" is the real
district championship
that everyone is chasing.

so far it has been a dream season.
we beat the team that was supposed to win;
not once, but twice.
and up until last tuesday,

we had managed, somehow, to beat everyone else.
even with that one defeat,
we still had a chance to tie,
if we only could manage to win every other game.
deep down, we thought there was still a chance to win it all.
there were still teams that could beat farmington,
and put us back in control of our own destiny.
elkton, in particular, had the size and speed, and the athletes to pull
it off.

last night we had our second exhibition game against the AHA.
you would have loved the pre-game talk....

"lets go out there, and give our very best.
let's use this game to get better....

and enjoy the moment for what it is.
you will see these guys on tv someday.
you might see some of them in the NBA.
and you can remember that you once played against them."

this time they took it easy on us,
and we only got beat 94-43.

that was just what it was.

what was important was the ride home.
we got a call from coach mike about halfway home.
elkton beat farmington last night.

we have only 3 district games left,
all at home.
we will be underdogs.
hell, we should be underdogs.
we don't match up against any of these teams.
but if we can find the magic, one game at a time,
we are only 3 games away from achieving the impossible.

there are things that are so wrong about high school sports.

but there are also things that are so right.
i wouldn't trade where we are right now for any other situation.
and i wouldn't want to go into these last 3 games
with any other group of guys.

one game at a time

we have four seniors on this year's team.
they have been playing basketball since the 3rd grade.

when you are young, it seems that the games and seasons
extend out in front of you forever.
when you are a senior,
suddenly you realize that your days are numbered.
when the tournaments approach,
you find yourself playing not for the game,
or even for the season,
but for your career.

we have one guy who might be able to extend his career at a small
college somewhere.
the others woke up one morning, to realize that this is it.
after playing, and loving, the game for most of their lives
the end of that life,
the end of childhood is staring them in the face.

people often decry the youth of today.
those people are selling their future short.
i have spent of lot of my cranky old life with these guys.
i have seen them at their best.
i have seen them at their worst.
i have watched them grow from boys into men.
our future is in good hands.

after our last game before christmas,
the seniors approached me in the locker room.
"you've been around a long time,"
one of them felt obligated to amend that to
"maybe forever"
and i reckon i have been here forever to them.
we have dads on our team that played for me.

"how do we stack up against the best teams the orange has had?"

like all of us, when our time is growing short,
they were wondering what would be their legacy.

at the time, i told them;
"all you have so far, is the best 'before christmas' season we have
ever had."
i did not have to finish.
one of them finished for me...

"the rest depends on what we do from here on out."
"yes. there is no banner for the team with the most potential."

last night i was sitting with the same four players before the game,
and i asked them;
"do you remember what you asked me before christmas?"
"you mean, how do we rate?"
"yes. well, i think we almost have an answer...

you take care of business in these last four games,
you will have had the best regular season in orange history."
"one game at a time."
it wasn't a question, it was a statement.
these guys are something special.
"that's the only way we can play them."

last night we played our cross county rival.
the same team that had ruined our tournament season last year.
the gym was packed, standing room only,
the doorways were jammed with fans,
and more people were out in the cafeteria that couldn't even fit in
the gym.

we had whaled the daylights out of them earlier in the season.
they were one of the first victims before everyone learned how we
wanted to run.
since that time, they had been one of the hottest teams in our old 1-
A district.
they came into our gym confident that things would be different
this time.

the early going was almost all them.
they had a good game plan,
controlling the pace on offense,
and running like mad to keep from getting beat down the floor on defense.
our opponent notched the first 5 points of the game,
and the visitors' bleachers roared their approval.

we fought back, and then our side of the stands got into the game.
with so many people crammed into our little gym,
the roar of the crowd drowned out the voices of coaches and players.
it was the first taste of the situation we hope to see a lot before the season ends.
the point guard has to be tuned in when to look at the bench for instructions.
and he can't just call out signals.
we have to use signs,
and everyone who gets the signal has to repeat it,
so that everyone will know.

about three minutes before the end of the first quarter,
we ignited our first real "run" of the game.
in the space of about 30 seconds their lead evaporated
and we took our first lead.
their coach called time out to stop our momentum.

they were desperate to keep the game slowed down.
our old cross country boys smelled blood in the water.
we came out with even greater intensity,
determined to bend them to our will.
we could see them gasping for air and holding their shorts...

it was like a shot of adrenaline.
our team has that killer instinct.

they had to burn another timeout in the second quarter,
and as we neared the half, they were hanging on by a thread.

a lot of people undervalue the "last shot" strategy in basketball.
approaching the half, it was a critical moment.
exhausted, but still clinging to contact on the scoreboard,
our opponent attempted to extend that last shot to its limit.
their hopes relied on shortening the clock as much as possible.
they could not afford to give up another run.

while we are simply not quick enough to press other teams,
the parameters are different when the other team is not trying to
attack the basket.
and even if we left some openings,
it was not to their tactical advantage to score.
they wanted to run out the final minutes on one end of the court.
that meant we could afford to extend our pressure.
it meant we could raise the intensity yet another level.
against the AA teams we have played all season,
it has often been us milking that last minute or two,
to avoid the danger of a run that put the game out of reach.
not this night.
it is a lot harder to control the ball, when you aren't attacking the
basket.
people who have never played have no idea how hard that can be.
it is harder still when you are physically exhausted.

we blew it open in the last minute,
and went to the locker room riding on a 16 point lead.

there were few adjustments to be made at the half.
but i had spotted one that was worth making
(in case you haven't noticed, i am always excited when i have a
contribution of any value)
they had slowed (but not stopped) our running game in the first
half,
but they were flooding defense to the ball side to do it.
we could send a flyer deep and pass long and cross court
to attack the defense from behind.
a few good kicks to the kidneys ought to be enough to break the
game wide open.

it was the kind of adjustment that could ordinarily be made during play.
but the deafening crowd noise and hectic pace of the game had made communication difficult.

they came out and valiantly attempted to make one last stand.
they even burned another timeout.
but having a new front opened to their rear proved to be too much.
they were soon waving the universal white flag of basketball,
running in 5 subs at once, from the deep bench.
the fourth quarter was played by both teams' jayvees with a running clock.
they had important games left to play in their own district,
and chose to save their frontline players for another day.

handshake lines can be difficult.
their disappointment was plainly visible.
they had come in with a good game plan, and played hard.
i felt bad for them.
but sometimes it is best to just shake hands and let people go to the locker room to regroup.

later, i saw their best player (a senior himself, having played the last game of a long and fierce rivalry)
he was talking to some of their people before he left for home.
that seemed the right time.
i went over and shook his hand (for real this time)
"good luck in the tournament. y'all have a good team, i think you can win your district."
the smile i got back was genuine, too.
"we're gonna try... good luck to you guys, too."

on the way out, i saw some of our guys getting ready to leave.
they were already talking about friday's opponent.
this game was over, the time for celebration was past.
The scoreboards have been set back to zeroes
and there is just one game to think about now.

one game that we have to win.

the tournament starts early

this was a big game for us tonight.
and a scary one.
with only 3 games left in the regular season,
our tournament started early this year.

i have run thru the "math" in my head a hundred times.
we might have started the season picked to finish winless and last
in our district.
we might have come in with a goal of just beating someone
(anyone)
but things did not turn out quite the way they looked on paper.

we won that one game.
then we won another, and another, and another....

coming into the last week of the season,
we sit in a tie for "2nd" in our district,
with a game still left to play against the team we are tied with.
they are also our only district loss.

we had to win all 3 of our remaining games,
and we would get a first round bye in the district tournament.
it would also put us in the opposite bracket from AHA.

that is very important.
the AHA will not lose in the tournaments.
they will win the state.
to do otherwise would be a failure of epic proportions...

i don't think they could lose in AA competition, even if they tried.

but there is a twist to modern-day tournaments in our state.
at the district and regional, it is not only the champions that
advance.
state association says that is because the best two teams might be
in the same district.

i think we all know that it is for the extra revenue,
but that is not important.
with our bye, we only have to win one district tournament game to
reach the finals.
there we will lose to AHA.
We need to avoid the extra games at all costs.
We have to play at an insane level to win against these bigger,
more athletic teams.
but we would advance in the opposite bracket in the regionals.
if we win two games in the regionals, we would make the finals
where we would again lose to AHA.

but the region's second place team travels to another region
winner's home court,
and plays in what is called the substate.
win there, and you are going to the state.

our situation when we took the court tonight was really simple.
we had to win 7 straight games to make it to state.
if we lose any one, we either get eliminated, or get thrown into the
same bracket as AHA.
and our season is over.

our task would not be an easy one.
we faced arno tonight, the only team in our district that we can
match up with.
if we could win tonight, and that was not a little if,
we would be huge underdogs in every other game we played.

to be honest, i find it hard to believe we are in this situation.
i was there for our games.
i saw it happen,
but i still can hardly believe we have won all these games.
coach mike even commented tonight;
"you know, i watch the tapes and catch myself thinking; 'how did
we beat these people?'"
but that is what this team does.
they aren't big, or fast, or quick.
they aren't much to look at.

they don't scare you when they take the floor.
if you took all the players in the district and picked a team,
our guys would be waiting in the player pool for a long time.
this team is not impressive to look at, individually.
together, they just win games.

tonight's game was also the classic "trap" game.
the kids know what we have ahead of us.
it is not so easy to reach an emotional peak for a beatable
opponent,
with so many giants waiting in the immediate future.
and for our opponent, arno, this game would make their season.
they came into the season knowing it was a down year...

but at least they could count on beating the little bitty team in
orange.

now little bitty orange was sitting at the top of the heap,
and they could make their season by ruining ours.
we were the one team left on their schedule that they match up
with physically.
the coaches knew they would come in with everything they had.
the players knew it, too.
but it is so hard to get up for the winnable game,
with so many giants waiting in the immediate future.

we took the early lead, like a favored team should.
but we could not shake arno loose.
we'd build a lead,
until we just needed one more little run to break it open.
and arno would come storming back.
we had leads as big as 16 during the first half.
but went into halftime only up by 7.

i know this script well.
we had been the scrappy rascals that wouldn't go away all year.
we did not want the final act to come out the same as ours,
with the underdog pulling off the upset at the end.

they had their moments in the third quarter.
we'd pull ahead, until we were almost to break it open.
they would come back yet again.
their players were putting heart and soul into this game.

early in the last quarter,
they battled to within 5.
it was a tense juncture in the game for us on the bench.
the team just couldn't seem to get in a rhythm,
and our opponent was red-hot,
sinking ridiculous shots.
that is what happens when you have nothing to lose.

but we were running in fresh players to finish the game.
we had worked our minutes chart and our long bench well.
arno's players were getting near the end of their tether.
we made another run, and got a little breathing room,
and as the clock ticked under 4 minutes, i thought to myself;
"if we get one more stop, i'm gonna suggest 20 passes"

we got the stop,
and as the team came back down the floor
before I could say anything,
coach mike called out "20!"

sometimes i think he is a genius.

it was the same story as so many of our games.
they were too tired to chase,
and had too much foul trouble to foul.

and we run our 20 passes well.
we should.
we practice it often.

as the clock ticked past 2 minutes,
we saw them send 5 young guys to check into the game.
the white flag was out.
coach mike called timeout, and we ran in our young guys to play it

out.
it was important to get those guys on the floor.
they work hard every day,
without their contributions in practice,
we would be a much lesser team.
and we might not have another game situation this season,
when we could put them in.

now we are 17-2, and our magic number is 6.

tuesday is a monster game.
we play farmington.
our only district loss.
they are so athletic, and so incredibly quick.
they have a lineup of guys who can dunk.
a lot of our players can touch the rim.
coach mike and i talked game plan long after the game was over,
and the fans had gone home.
he will spend the weekend watching film,
and trying to figure out any advantages we have,
any weakness we might exploit....

even if they are imaginary.

on paper we don't have a chance.
but they don't play the game on paper.
they play it on the floor.
our floor this time.
and this is not just a game.
it is our season.
for our seniors, it is their career.
the tournament started early this year.

the big game

i promised myself i would pass along the outcome.
win or lose.
and that is what i will do.

it was the biggest game of the year.
the biggest game our players have ever played.
our opponent, farmington, was big, and fast, and strong.
and it was their biggest game of the year.
we had each battled our way thru a long, hard season,
and our paths had converged at this point in time.
we were tied at the top of the district.
they had but one loss, and we had one loss.
our loss had been to them.

at the end of the night, one of us would be alone.
one of us would control their own destiny.
one would be hoping for help.
looking for miracles.

the smart money was on them.
we are not big. we are not fast, and we are not strong.
we have a good coach.
coach mike is a canny veteran of many of these campaigns.
they have a good coach.
he is young, but he has proven his merit
by the team he puts on the floor.

we had only one thing going for us.
our guys win games they are supposed to lose.
they have done it all year.
that is why we were in the big game.
they have done it at every level.
but this night,
this night the stakes are the highest they have ever been.
this night, for our four seniors,
their careers in orange were on the line.

the game had weighed heavy on my mind,
since the last biggest game of the year.
this is the time of year when every game is the biggest game of the
year.
and all that comes from winning the biggest game of the year,
is another game that is even bigger.
there is only one game that ends it all with victory.
everyone who plays the game understands this truth.
every team, save one, ends their season with tears.

we had our game plan.
much of it was the same as last time.
the goals were the same.
but we had made adjustments in how we hoped to accomplish
those goals.
if you only do what you did before.
you get what you got before.
we did not like what we got before.
before, we got beat.

we had tweaked our defense.
changed some assignments, adjusted our focus.
the last game, their #15 had destroyed our defense.
with the quickness and agility of a big cat,
he had penetrated again and again.
and once he collapsed our defense, he either scored,
or dished off to team-mates for easy baskets.
he was not the high scorer, but he was the key to their victory.

we gave blake the unenviable assignment of stopping 15.
last time, blake had been coming back from an injury.
blake is not a big scorer. he doesn't get any headlines.
he never tops the box-scores.
but blake is worth his weight in gold.
when we have a tough defensive assignment, inside or out,
it falls to blake.
with his tenacious defensive play, his rebounding, his hustle;
with his unselfishness,

and his quiet leadership by example ,
blake would be a valuable player on any team.

and blake has one other characteristic that coaches value.
he plays his best games in the biggest games.
there was no guarantee he could stop 15;
or even slow him down.
but, if anyone could, it was blake.
making him the lynchpin of our defensive plan was an easy choice.

on offense, the plan was simple.
against a bigger, stronger, quicker opponent,
we were going to go right at their strength.
last time our shot selection was not good.
we took too many long shots under pressure.
we have good outside shooting,
but we need space to get good shots.
the only way to get that space was to attack the body.
if we could not cause pain in the paint,
our offense would struggle again.
last time, our inside guys had been intimidated after a few blocked
shots.
we had lost our aggressiveness.
you cannot succeed at basketball if you are not aggressive.
the fear of failure assures failure.
everyone understood what they had to do.
we had to pound the ball inside.
and then we had to score it.
we had to strap it on, and go right at them.
sometimes there is not a trick or technique to teach.
sometimes the only thing you can tell a player is;
"you just have to get it done."

and then there is transition; the running game.
we have made a lot of hay in transition this year.
but so has farmington.
they also love to run the floor.
and with their speed, they run the floor like cheetahs.
this time it was us putting extra emphasis on getting back.

it was imperative that we not only defend against the running
game,
but we had to keep attacking, ourselves.
last time, we had fought to pretty much a draw in the running
game.
i felt like their players sometimes relied a little too much on
athleticism.
sometimes they left a window.
those windows were small, and they weren't open long.
so we needed to be ready to exploit every opportunity we were
afforded.
and we had to keep the pressure on.

they have decent numbers,
but we run a long bench, and we run it according to plan.
last time, some of our younger players had been physically
overwhelmed,
and we could not keep them in the game.
when you run a short bench, you get tired.
even when you have your guys in as good condition as we have.
those young guys had been thru some wars since then.
if there was any value in our "games" against AHA,
it was the hardening of our young warriors.
they had to come thru for us this night, and hold their own on the
floor.

the job this night was simple.
every man on our team had to play the game of his life.
sometimes, your best is not good enough.
sometimes you have to play better than that...

the gym was electric.
the stands were packed for a tuesday night game,
and the fans knew what was at stake as much as the players.
the air crackled with energy.
once the ball was put in play,
the sound was not going to let up until the issue was decided.

the early going was like two heavyweights trading punches.

first one team got a few points ahead,
and then the other.
blake came thru, like we knew he would.
everywhere 15 wanted to go,
blake was already there.
blake thwarted him at every turn.
but it wasn't like farmington was a one trick pony.
they hit us from all directions.
we could not totally stop them,
but we held our own.

on the other end of the floor,
we pounded at the middle.
we won some battles, and we lost some battles.
but we were getting the inside scoring we had to have.
we forced their defense to collapse inside,
and opened up windows for our shooters to bomb from long range.

the roar of the crowd never stopped,
it just shifted from one side to the other, as first one team,
and then the other,
made big plays....

and in a game like this, every play is big.

crowd noise is a funny thing.
you can't really hear it.
in some ways, it is as if no one is in the gym except the teams.
but you can feel it.
and it certainly alters what you can do.

at one point, i saw an farmington player get lost behind our
defense.
he was sliding in under the basket behind our back line,
unseen.
"BASELINE, BASELINE, BASELINE!"

in november, my shouts would have alerted the defense,
and someone would have picked him up.

on a night like this,
i might as well have been whistling in a tornado.

a lightning quick pass pierced our defense like a dart,
and the lost man laid the ball in.
the lead changed hands,
and the roar switched sides of the gym...

for the moment.

for all the game planning you do,
the game is often shaped by the vagaries of chance.
we had gotten a lot of shots blocked,
but we had continued to attack the middle.
and 15 was also a stalwart on defense...

inside defense.

halfway thru the second quarter, he picked up his third foul.
shot-blocking is a mixed blessing.
it can prevent scores.
you hope it intimidates your opponent,
and stops them from attacking inside.
but there are going to be fouls called.
you hope the fouls don't fall on someone you have to have on the
floor.

our relentless pounding the ball inside had paid off.
15 had to go to the bench to protect his last 2 fouls.

with 15 out of the equation,
the situation changed.
sure, we had prevented him from dominating the offense,
but only at the cost of leaving them other openings.
with 15 gone,
we could turn our attention to shutting the rest of the team down.
and on offense,
suddenly the dominance in the paint swung to our side.

we made good use of the new paradigm on the floor,
and by halftime, we had opened up a double digit lead.

the game was far from over.
15 would be back,
and we knew they were next door, making adjustments.
it was a happy situation, that most of our adjustments were
anticipatory adjustments.
one of the benefits of having been in so many games,
we had a good idea of the sort of adjustments to expect.
so we went over those things with the team.
our biggest change;
we no longer would be trying to evade 15 on offense.
we wanted to go right at him.
he is a great player, and he would win a lot of battles.
but he was one foul from having to go cautious in order to stay in
the game.
he was 2 fouls from being gone.
without him, the game became entirely winnable.

our last advice to the team, before going back out;
"weather the storm."
farmington was going to come out on a mission.

the third quarter opened as we knew it would.
farmington made a charge, cutting into our lead.
then we came back with a flurry of our own.
the game returned to the see-saw affair it had been in the first
quarter.
only this time it was see-sawing around a 10 point margin,
not zero.

as the battle raged,
the tell-tale signs of fatigue began to show.
that facet was going our way, too.
the young guys had come thru,
holding their own on the floor.
and we were able to work our careful rotation.
as the third quarter wound down,

much of our front line was on the bench resting up for the final push.
and the fighting was still going on around our 10 point margin.

as the 4th quarter approached, farmington mounted one final charge.
15 had been hampered by the need to be careful of fouls.
it was time to let it all hang out.
they could feel the district title slipping thru their fingers,
and they mounted one last, desperate charge to take it back.

they were still the physically dominant team,
and they started to make it pay.
the lead slipped under 10,
and we had no answering charge.
we had our own foul problems,
blake had 3 of his own.

they kept chipping away,
and we kept on struggling to hold on.
then the second turning point arrived.
15 was all over one of our guards coming down the floor.
he had stripped us of the ball several times already.
much of their comeback was built on making it difficult for us to keep the ball.
but trying to steal the ball has the same risk as blocking shots.
you are going to commit some fouls.

15 was whistled for his 4th.
our bench was jubilant....

and then 15 lost his composure.
he ran down the floor and jumped up in the air,
swinging his fist in frustration.
and he did it right in front of the official who had just called the foul.
he made such a display, that he received a technical foul...

and technical fouls count against your foul count.

in one fell swoop, he was gone.

his 4th foul would have been damaging to his team.
the 5th was fatal.
to compound matters, their coach had a momentary lapse,
and got a technical of his own.
they have no "tug on your shirt" coach.
that is another of my jobs.
in those moments of high stress that are part of big games,
i tug on coach mike's shirt;
"don't worry about it. it is done. we have to keep playing."
he probably hates me for it sometimes, but it is my job.
we shot a long line of free throws,
hit them all, got back our double digit lead
and the game was, for all intents and purposes, over.

we are alone at the top.
it felt like nothing else for a good 30 minutes.

then we had to start thinking ahead.
we have 2 days to get ready for thompson's station.
they are way bigger than us.
they are the biggest team in the district.
there is no way we should win that game.
last time, we shocked them at the very end.
they are going to want us bad...

and it is the biggest game of the year.

i thought a lot about AHA last night.
i have been guilty of feeling a lot of animosity towards them.
but last night, i realized i feel kind of sorry for them.
they will never know the feeling we had last night.
sure, they will be happy to win another state "championship"
they will get to put another trophy in their trophy case,
and they will get to buy themselves rings...

but what will it really mean?

they went out of state last weekend,
and played a team that could match up with them.
they lost in overtime.
afterwards, their coach blamed us.
"beating people like we have been beating them,
you don't get much experience in these situations."
he also said that, while they did not "accept" defeat,
that game was not important.
what was important was winning their state championship.

the one that they can only lose by a monumental failure.

is that the message?
they have lost twice in real games this year.
against teams that can match up, they have been only a so-so team.
but what really counts is knocking over the tomato cans they have
lined up.
their season is built around beating up on weaklings?

coach mike once commented that he did not understand why they
did it.
"what is the fun in playing games, if you can't lose?"
i know what he means.
winning is the objective,
and winning is fun.

but it doesn't mean much,
unless you know you could also lose.
and winning the games you are supposed to lose;
that is the greatest feeling of all.

sports is not about the wins and the championships.
it is about the quest, and the challenge.

our guys won't get rings at the end of the season.
sooner or later, our time together will end with tears.
but, until then, we get to play the biggest game of the season...

over and over until we finally meet someone whose biggest game is bigger than ours.

i wouldn't trade that for all the trophies and rings that money can buy.

burning barns

we had played so many biggest games of the year already.
but last friday was going to be one more.
finally, we had reached the last game of the regular season.
the second season was almost complete.

our opponent was thompson's station.
in theory, it should be an easier game,
thompson's station was next to last in the district.
but thompson's station was a particularly difficult matchup for us.
as the smallest team in the district,
we had our difficulties dealing with size;
and thompson's station is the biggest team in the district.
if they could get the ball inside,
we could do little to prevent them from scoring.

we had beaten them at their place,
but it was a game in which we had trailed until the final minutes,
and then pulled together a miracle at the end.

it had been a season of miracles.
i wondered if we could manufacture one more.
the lead-up to the game got off to a bad start,
when alex was lost for the season...

mononucleosis.

it was a serious blow.
alex is as close as we come to presenting a matchup problem for
anyone.
back when these guys were in the 6th grade,
alex had been a tiny little guy, and played point guard.
he was tiny,
but he was tough as a strip of leather.

i will never forget our game in the 6th grade against mcfadden,
alex was on the receiving end of the hardest screen i have seen at

any level.
one tactic used in basketball is the screen (or pick)
where an offensive player sets up in the path of a defensive player,
and another offensive player leads the defensive player to run
headlong into the screener.
you might not be able to block on the move, like in football.
but neither do you have to get out of the way.
a hard pick can rattle a player's teeth.

it is vitally important,
in a man defense,
that the player who is guarding a man who sets up for a screen
call out that information to his team-mates.

high school players are usually somewhat competent at that.
no one wants to be responsible for his team-mate getting his bell
rung...

in the 6th grade the guys are just learning.

alex was a tenacious defender,
and generally guarded the other team's point guard.
being tiny has few advantages in basketball.
one of those advantages is that little guys are difficult to dribble
around.
alex was routinely a torment to the other team's point,
disrupting offenses before they could get started.

against mcfadden, alex had been wreaking his customary havoc,
and they called timeout to set up a play to deal with him.
when they came back out,
their point dribbled in a wide arc around the perimeter of our
defense...

as fast as he could go.
alex shadowed him every step,
also running full speed.
their biggest post player (thick as a tree trunk)
quietly slipped out and waited; braced for impact.

the man guarding him should have been responsible for calling out;
"SCREEN, SCREEN!"
he just watched the play unfold,
not really grasping what was about to happen.

alex hit that screen going full bore.
focused on his man, he never saw it coming.
it was like a bug hitting a windshield.

play was stopped while i went out to check on alex.
he just lay on the floor, dazed, in a tangle of little skinny arms and
legs.
when i got there,
i could see big tears welled up in his eyes...

the first thing he said was;
"i'm ok."

we still had a long way to go to master it.
but i never again had to explain to that group why we call out
screens.

alex remained the smallest kid on the team until his sophomore and
junior years.
he shot up to 6 feet tall,
and at a school our size, 6 feet means you almost have to be a post.
with his ball-handling skills, and outside shooting,
other teams at least had to think about whether to defend alex with
a post or a guard.
depending on which way they went,
we could move him around in our offense,
and sometimes get a mismatch.
that had been huge,
because we have spent the season on the wrong end of almost
every mismatch.
and now alex was gone.

his replacement, if you can consider alex replaceable, was younger
and 6 inches shorter.

not the best way to approach our biggest size mismatch.
alex was also a vital cog in our rotation scheme.
we had a lot of concerns going into the game.

being the last home game of the year,
we had our senior night festivities.
i will be honest.
i hate senior night...

just like homecoming, or any of the other "traditions" that distract
our players.
but, you gotta have that stuff or the mommies will complain.

 being senior night, we made a deal with the other team.
alex would get to wear his uniform, and "start" the game.
his parents would get to hear his name called out on the
loudspeaker one last time.
then, if the other team won the tip, they would immediately throw
the ball out of bounds,
so alex could come out.
(then we would give it right back)
if we won the tip, the officials would immediately blow the
whistle,
and we would use a time out to replace him.

i just sort of assumed we would be giving the ball back.
we hadn't won a tip all season,
and we really had no chance against thompson's station.
they had about a foot height advantage.
but their coach doesn't miss a trick.
they didn't even try to get the tip, and we had to burn a timeout.

it did not seem that important at the time.
we hadn't used all our timeouts in a game yet...

it would be important.
we would really wish we had that timeout before the night was
over.

as i watched alex come to the bench,
this sad look on his face,
i was surprised to feel tears welling up in my own eyes.
there were hugs and wet eyes with his team-mates.
i shook his hand and put an arm around his shoulder.
i had no words. some situations transcend the need for words.

this was not the way alex wanted to end it all.
it was not the way it should have ended.
alex had been playing for the orange since the sixth grade.
and just like that, without warning, it was over.

for me, it was like the end of an era.
alex's older brother had played from the early 1990's
until his own senior year ended in tears around 2005.
(the elder A went to the air force academy. we are proud of the
kind of guys that play for us)
there has been one or both in our system for 20 years,
and i am going to miss them.
their dad played here in the 1980's.
somehow, it seems unlikely i will be around for another
generation.

then i found it advisable to study my clipboard for a few moments.
i needed to compose myself.
there was a big game to be played.

thompson's station surprised us by coming out in a zone defense.
last game they went man the whole way,
and it gave us a lot of difficulty because of the size differential.
i am not sure what the thinking was,
but they surprised us coming out in a zone.

not that we minded.
against the zone we were able to spring our outside shooters loose
for open shots.
we ran out to an 11-2 lead,
and i felt relieved.

unfortunately,
whatever the plan had been, their coach was smart enough to
abandon it.
they returned to their cursed man defense,
and we started to struggle looking for good shots.
the tide reversed,
and it was thompson's station who went on a 14-2 run.

the rest of the half was spent fighting for our lives.
with our size disadvantage accentuated,
we had a lot of trouble keeping them from getting the ball inside.
once it was inside, they were simply too big to stop.

for our part,
every man was dogged by a bigger defender.
we had to work our butts off
(and use a lot of screens!)
just to get off any shots.

i'm not sure how we managed it,
but we stayed in the game.
thompson's station would pull away to a small lead,
 then we would go into a frenzy and catch back up.

there weren't many adjustments to make at the half,
for either team.
they had a decided advantage,
and it didn't seem possible that we could continue to hang in the
game.
we had our backs to the wall,
but there weren't many things left to try.
our remaining inside players all had foul problems.
and we had put too many minutes on several guys.
we have a long bench, but the players are not big.
it was all we could do to keep a lineup on the floor that was not
physically overwhelmed.
the second half was all out war.
they could not build a lead over 3 or 4 points,
and we were lucky to get a one point lead here and there.

as the game rolled into the final two minutes,
our situation was dire.
they were ahead, and the lead was swinging between 1-2 and 3-4
points.
one of our big guys had fouled out,
and we could no longer stop them from getting the ball inside.
we were somehow squeezing out a basket every possession,
to get back within one score.
but we could not stop them from scoring.
they called a timeout.
we knew they were setting up their final play...

our guess was that it would be their version of "20."
i was relieved.
the advantage of size is markedly less handling the ball around
midcourt,
than it is down around the basket.
i honestly did not think they could keep the ball from us for that
long.
we talked about fouling, but decided against it,
so we went out playing straight.

it was the right decision.
we got a steal and a layup within 20 seconds,
and the game was tied.

then we called timeout. our last.
we have not pressed anyone all season.
we can't. we simply lack the quickness to press.
it would get us killed.

but we have a press.
for emergencies.

this was an emergency.
if we did not do something,
they would simply take the ball down, punch it inside,
and score.

remarkably, they seemed to have had no idea what was coming,
and when we showed press, not everyone on their team set up un
their press break.
to make matters worse,
they threw the ball to their biggest post,
and when the man he was supposed to pass to was not in position,
he put the ball on the floor with a dribble.

now, he had been destroying us inside all night,
and he has good ball handling skills.
but his size and ours was not to his advantage dribbling at
midcourt.
have i ever mentioned that it is difficult to dribble around little
guys?

as soon as he put the ball on the floor,
midgets swarmed him from both sides.
he deftly maneuvered the ball away from the first,
and the second,
but zig-zagging the ball from side to side,
it hit his foot and started to bounce away.
the big guy reached for the loose ball, to pick it up,
but our men were a lot closer to the floor than he was.

a second later we were on the way to shooting a layup and taking
the lead.

for the past 3 minutes of play,
every time we took a lead we had been praying for;
"just one stop"
if we could get the ball with a lead,
we could run our 20 offense.
our only advantage, with our diminutive team, was out on the floor
away from the basket.
every time, we did not get that stop.

but things are a lot different when the clock is winding down.
under pressure, a thompson's station player hurried a shot.

not a bad shot, but he missed it.
we weren't able to pull down the rebound clean,
but we kept it alive, and came up with the ball.

this was it.
after all the adversity, we had the game in our hands.
ours to win.

as the guys brought the ball up,
coach mike was yelling for "20"
i was yelling for "20"
we wanted to yell for timeout,
but we had used that up way back at the beginning of the game.

i haven't mentioned it,
because we hardly notice it most of the time,
but the volume of sound in the gym was like a physical force.
the players could no more hear us than the man in the moon.
our point guard knew to look,
and he got the signal,
which he passed along to the other players....

all but one.
one, who was playing in place of alex.
his most dominant characteristic as a player all year had been his
heads up play.
but, looking across the floor, he seemed to be in a trance.
he had not been in a situation this intense before.

four of our players lined up for 20.
one was floating around in the corner with a blank expression on
his face.
with no timeouts, there was nothing we could do,
except keep yelling "20" and hope.

without one in position,
we were unable to work the ball across the top of the offensive
end,
and had to take it to the corner.

this time, it was the thompson's station coach desperately calling
to his players
(who had no chance of hearing him)
they needed to foul, so we could not just run out the clock.
from the corner, we could not get the ball back out to the top,
so our corner man dribbled towards the basket,
where their big guy was waiting.
for just a moment i was afraid he would try a hopeless layup,
but, spotting the lost player, who was still floating around in the
opposite corner in his trance,
he passed it out.

with all my being, i willed the lost man to simply bring the ball
back out top.
there was no defense on him,
thompson's station being forced to collapse on the ball, where ever
it went.
but my force of will was insufficient.
he shot the ball.

a wide open 3 is not generally a bad shot.
we had not got very many looks like that since thompson's station
came out of their zone.
but it was a horrible shot in this situation.

we won the game at thompson's station on an ill-advised shot that
went in.
i tried to will this one in,
but it was not to be.
the shot clanked off,
thompson's station got the rebound,
and brought it down to try to tie.
this time they made no mistakes, and the game was tied.

playing from the front, we still had one more advantage.
there were 23 seconds remaining when we got the ball.
we had the chance to take the last shot...

win or overtime.

if only we had a timeout to set it up.

but we didn't.
and again, 4 of the players understood what we wanted.
one was still lost in his trance.
thompson's station was still overplaying everything,
and when the lost man got the ball with an open lane to the basket
at 10 seconds,
he drove to the basket.
their post, a good foot taller, was waiting for him.

in a last shot situation,
you want to take your shot with less than 5 seconds left.
(unless it is an uncontested layup)
this is to make sure your last shot is actually the last shot.

our guy realized that he had no chance of getting his shot past the
much taller waiting defender,
and tried to go under the basket to shoot a reverse layup
(using the rim to shield the ball from the defense)

he was too out of step to make it,
and ended up shooting the ball off the bottom of the rim.
it bounced off his head and out of bounds.
now it was thompson's station with 8 seconds to get off the last
shot.
win or overtime.

again, we rued not having a timeout to set our defense.
and thompson's station got the ball close enough for a good shot at
the basket.
luckily for us, it rimmed out,
and we prepared for overtime.

if the final stages of regulation play were desperate,
overtime was worse.
it goes without saying that thompson's station won the tip this
time.
and started off by taking a lead.

somehow, we managed to answer.
and every time they scored, we came back to tie it up.
even after our other "big" player fouled out,
and we were left looking like a middle school team playing against
a high school,
our guys refused to let the game get away.
we were surviving on the one thing that has made this team special
since elementary school.
the sheer will to win.

but we were left without the means to stop our opponent.
we needed them to make a mistake.

that mistake came with 8 seconds left.
thompson's station scored to take yet another lead with only about
15 seconds left.
we had no time to work for the shot we wanted,
and will launched a desperation 3 under heavy pressure.
the shot missed,
but their defender knocked will flying.
we had 3 free throws to take the lead.
will is our best shooter.
this was the situation all his work has been for...

and his first free throw hit the front of the rim and bounced off.
he hit the second, and we called timeout.
you get an extra timeout for overtime,
and we had not wasted this one.
if we missed the last free throw, the game was pretty well over.
our guys knew they would have to get a miracle rebound,
or foul immediately.
what we worked on was the 8 second defense.
we did not want thompson's station to get another good shot.

will sunk the free throw to tie the game.
our defense came off just as planned.
we made them throw it in short,
and then turned the ball several times coming up the floor.
the seconds were melting away.

we gave them nothing in the middle of the floor,
forcing them to pass the ball out by the sideline,
about 40 feet from the basket.

they didn't even get off a real shot,
just a desperation, two-handed, sideways heave
in the general direction of the goal.

the horn sounded as the ball arced thru the air,
and missed the basket by a good two feet...

unfortunately, it hit the backboard instead,
and ricocheted cleanly thru for the winning points.
on this night we were the stunned losers,
and another team finished the night in jubilant celebration.
what an unexpected path the season had taken,
when victory over us would make another team's season.
three months ago, victories over us were considered a given.

and so the second season ended.
with us standing at 18-3, and needing help.
we had our game to clinch a possible path to the state,
and we lost.
now we needed someone to knock off farmington
and give us a coin toss of a chance at regaining that path.

we got our help,
and we won our coin toss.
the third season begins with us 4 games from the promised land.
we are the longest of long shots.
we were hopelessly outmanned with everybody there.
without alex, victory seems impossible.
i know in my brain that we have no chance.

but in my heart i only know that the scoreboard reads zero to zero.
and that tomorrow will be what we make it.

friday we play in the biggest game of the year.

survivor basketball

so i went to our last practice before the big game.

jesse was not there.
he has mono, and is gone for the season.

coach mike told me, with a wry smile;
"he is going to another doctor today. he wants a second opinion."

that would be jesse.
he doesn't expect another doctor to tell him he isn't sick.
he just wants one to tell him he can play.
nothing stops jesse.
if he broke a leg, he'd just tape it up and play.

i can't believe it.
another post player gone.
our best inside scorer and rebounder...

we were already smaller than anyone else,
and now we lose 2/3 of our inside players?

i asked coach mike if we were playing survivor basketball...

"after every game we vote a player off?"

just so you will know.
there is no way we win the game tomorrow.

but the scoreboard still reads zero to zero.
i reckon we'll take the guys that are left
and have a go at it.

fatigue

it was a long drive home last night,
getting here after midnight.

and it was an early morning this morning.
it is funny how emotion can be as exhausting as physical exertion.
and how a long hard season can wear on you.

there was great news when i arrived at the tournament site.
jesse was going to play, after all.
things have sure changed with mono.
back in my senior year of HS,
our outstanding girls' team was wrecked when their point guard
got mono.
she was just out for the year.

jesse had found that other doctor he was looking for.
an MRI showed his spleen to not be enlarged.
he was told he could safely play.

as it turns out, he could only play about 2 minutes at a stretch.
but the emotional boost for coaches and players alike was
tremendous.
and when he did play, he played like his old self.

and getting jesse back was not our only cause to celebrate.
alex was at the game watching.
i think he is campaigning to get to go to the same doctor jesse went
to.
he says he feels better, and he looks a lot better.

having everyone there was a huge lift.
these guys love each other,
the way only a team forged under fire can.

it has been a long, hard season,
having to play out of our heads every night.

but you couldn't tell it by our guys.
we had been intense in practice,
and looking around the locker room,
you could see it in the faces,
and feel it in the air.
we had come here to win a game.

we trailed 3-2 early on,
and then scored a couple of baskets to ease out front.
then it was the same old story.
no matter what our opponent did,
we scratched and clawed to answer.
our guys protect a lead like banty hens protect their chicks.

and when jesse went in for his short stints,
you could see everyone pick it up another level.

we had been talking about our personnel losses all week.
and in the locker room before the game,
coach mike put it on the line.
"we have a lot of points and rebounds to make up.
everyone has to do their part.
you have to do everything you have been doing...

and then a little more."

and that is how the guys were playing.
we fought for every rebound, like it was the last rebound of the last
game of our lives.
our opponent had great outside shooters.
ordinarily we would not play much zone defense,
which is vulnerable to outside shooting.
but with the holes in our lineup, we had to play mostly zone to
protect the middle.
in practice, we had worked on our zone against 2 extra
offensive players on the perimeter,
running long, hard drills,
scrambling to keep the inside packed,
and still close out the shooters before they could get a good,

open look.
"you have to see the pass. you have to beat the ball to the open
man."
it isn't really possible.
but sometimes the assignment is that you just have to get the job
done.

and that was how we played the game.
every man kept the needle above the red line, every second.

at the half, up by 7, our team was gassed.
the coaches got together out in the hall before we went into the
locker room.
this is something we always do.
we go over the situation, the adjustments.
we prepare for what we will go over during our few minutes.
a good staff funnels everything thru the head coach,
then, during the brief periods you can communicate,
the players get a single message from a single voice.

way back at the beginning of the season,
during our first impossible win,
we had gone into this same locker room, in this same situation.
it has very limited seating, only a single bench.
the jayvees had run in ahead of the varsity and grabbed all the
seats.
we had to toss them, so the guys playing could get as much rest as
possible.

later i had talked to a couple of the jayvee leaders,
and told them;
"you have to take charge of the locker room, when it is like this.
make sure we keep the seats open for the guys that are playing."

when we walked in the locker room at the half last night,
the varsity players were all lined up on the single bench, leaning
against the wall.
the jayvees were standing.
i looked around until i saw the guys i had talked to, all that time

ago,
and i nodded.
they just grinned.

as we left the locker room, i was next to one of them;
"good job."
"oh, everyone knew what to do."

his momma might think he is not getting anything,
when he is not on the floor very often...

he is getting everything.
accept the blame for failure. distribute the credit for success.
when his day comes, he will be ready to lead his team on the floor.

after coach mike had gone over everything,
i got to add my piece.
usually i add nothing.
that way, when I have something to say, maybe it will mean
something.
there wasn't much to add.
certainly no x's and o's.
"16 minutes guys. everything we want is only 16 minutes away."

we were unusually long in the locker room.
these games are life and death of a team and a season.
our opponent was gone even longer,
not returning to the floor until the ref was waiting with the
game ball in his hand.
we weren't the only team with everything on the line.

they made the run we expected.
we staved it off.

and then about halfway thru the quarter, magic happened.
every once in a while, a combination of players on the floor just
clicks.
every pass is perfect.
every shot finds nothing but net.

they anticipate every move on defense,
and time every jump perfectly.
5 minds seem to meld into one,
and the team acts as a single organism.
the result is an explosion.

and it happens so fast that the score can get out of control in a
hurry.

magic happened last night,
and it was like a flash fire on the floor.
right in the middle, it came time for our rotation.
i tapped coach mike on the elbow and said;
"i know you don't want to do it now,
but we just hit 4 minutes."
coach mike just nodded.
when the fire went out,
we would make substitutions.

the other coach got caught.
for one thing it happened so fast.
for another, he had already burned too many timeouts,
dealing with the special stuff we had put in for this game.
when we started playing like a normal team again,
we were up by 21.

we rolled in the substitutes,
and i looked at the scoreboard.
we could not relax, just yet.
there was a job to finish.
but i knew we were going to win.

the game ended with both teams' jayvees on the floor.

we are 19-3 now.
we have to make that damned long drive again, and go thru the
formality of losing to AHA.
but we are the real district champions.
us.

the little team that wasn't supposed to win a single game.
and we are the last real high school team standing.
our goal for today is to lose by less than 50.
but we don't really control that.
it is a matter of what score they want to put up.

our minds are already on next week.
we don't know who we play yet,
but we can narrow it down to two teams.

they are both, on paper, vastly superior to us.
but, hell, who in AA ball isn't?

we do have one advantage.
whoever we play, their coach is going to have a hard time getting
his team to take us seriously.
that was how the season started in our district.
the other teams would laugh and joke when we walked on the
floor.
they have been taking us dam seriously for a while now.
it is going to be a relief to play someone who has never seen us
before.

i can even predict what whoever we play's coach will tell his team
after they watch our first tape.
"don't write this bunch off. they are 19-3. that doesn't happen by
accident."
good luck with that, coach.
when we watch our tapes, even we don't understand how we won.
(and we were there!)

but, that is what these guys do.
they are too small, too slow, and not very athletic.
all they do is win games.

if they win 2 more, they will match the farthest our team has ever
gone.
3 more, and we go to the promised land.

i know we can't do it.
but the dream lives on for at least one more game

the man behind the curtain

we played the championship "game" last night.
a lot of it was what i expected.
a lot of it was not.

back just after christmas we played AHA,
and they blew us out by 60.
it was never a game from the opening tip.

a few weeks ago,
we had the pleasure of playing them again.
we hung in there for about 2 minutes.
they beat us by 50.

last night we swapped leads for a quarter.
and pushed them almost until the half.
there is no reason we should swap leads for a quarter.
it is like running a miniature donkey in the kentucky derby,
and leading thru the first turn.

but we did.
of course, being pushed to our limits every night out makes us
better.
(that is why i would schedule an opponent like them, if i could, as
often as i could)
playing an endless string of cupcakes has not made them better.

oh, they ended up winning by 30.
the weight of all those athletes won out in the end.
but under pressure,
any pressure,
we got to see who is behind the curtain.

after the game, the kids said;
"boy, they are all about sportsmanship when they beat you by 60.
but they don't handle it very well if you play with them."
and it was true.

being challenged for a quarter hardly qualifies as adversity.
but even that, they handled poorly.
they whined at the officials,
made faces,
pouted,
ran their mouths,
and generally behaved in a manner that would not be acceptable on
our team.

i would hate to pay that kind of money to send my kid to school,
and all he gets is a ring,
and the knowledge of how to be polite...

as long as he wins in a blowout.

our guys want to play them again.
had they handled it like men, their aura might have remained
intact.
but that glimpse at what is behind the curtain changed things.
"they aren't supermen. they can be beat."

the teams we have faced so far have been enormous challenges.
but the teams that remain ahead are going to be tougher still.
tournaments weed out the weak.
and the challenges that remain will get bigger every game.
(not counting last night!)

we learned something last night, that could hold us in good stead.
we had to use a time out in the first quarter,
when they made a little run and we got rattled.

i could see will was all tore up,
and i told him to;
"relax. we aren't going to win this in the first quarter."
"but i want to win!"
"i want to win, too. but we aren't going to blow them off the
floor...

we just have to stay in it till the end."

after the game, we talked about it.
the teams we are playing now are too good to get them rattled.
they are not just good and talented,
they have been thru the winnowing process.
the teams that will fall apart under pressure are gone.

to beat a more physically talented opponent,
that is also a quality team,
we have to stay in the game, and win it at the end.
will gets it now.
we all get it.

one team got better last night.

we don't play again until saturday,
and we won't know the opponent until tuesday
(other tournaments have fallen behind, possibly weather related)

it's a long drive,
but we will have the privilege of seeing who gets to play our
ragged band, in person.

cheers and tears

we spent the week while the other tournaments were catching up wisely.
actually, we spent it the only way we could.
we practiced in the afternoons,
and went scouting at night.

we got a good look at the next hurdle on the road to state.
they weren't tremendously big.
but they could shoot the lights out.
i wasn't sure how much use i was on the scouting trips.
an infected tooth was at its worst,
and i had a hard time staying conscious during the games,
to say nothing of those long drives.

instead of a page of notes,
i had only a few scribblings.
but i did come away from the games with some impressions.
our upcoming opponent had 4 seniors, and a will to win.
we thought they were going to lose the last game before us.
they were down 10 in the 4th quarter.
but this was good basketball team
(probably why they boasted 22 wins)

we figured they had only seen tape on us.
and we wondered which tapes they had seen.
i knew one thing.
we might have labeled them "the shooters"
they had to be calling us the "what are they doing here?"

i did have one of those prescient moments.
or maybe just a rare lucid moment.
i commented on the way back;
"you know; we haven't pressed all year. we would get killed if we tried.
but i'm not sure we couldn't get away with red for a possession or two...

117

right at the end.
if we really needed it...

you know they won't be preparing for it."

coach mike agreed.
at the end of our last practice,
he started to call it a day,
then he told the guys;
"oh, one more thing we need to do"
we did something we hadn't done all year.
we worked our red press."
it didn't look good.
we don't have the people to press.
our other guys broke it with ease.
i told myself things might be different if it was a surprise.

on game day it was odd preparing for the first game.
all year there had been a game ahead of us.
the girls during the regular season,
and other games during the tournaments.
giving pre-game instructions
with only the sound of a nervous crowd gathering in the gym
outside our door...

that was different.

the game started out great.
teams in our district had been taking us serious for a while.
clearly, these guys had seen us on film.
we hadn't gotten a real chance to run in a bunch of games.
we toasted them for several snowbirds.
early in the second quarter we had pulled out to a 12 point lead.
our crowd was in full celebration
(and like any team making a tournament run, we were gaining
more fans every game)

they took a timeout early in the second,
and seemed to pull themselves together.

we were going to be a little tougher nut to crack than they had
expected.

at the half our lead was down to 6.
we made some adjustments on defense,
settling on the strategies that had worked best in the first half,
running various versions of our 2-3 zone,
and trapping their shooters.

they made their own adjustments.
our snowbirds went extinct in the second half.
but we kept running anyway.
in the games we had seen (live or on film) they only used 6
players.
with our rotation, the pressure had to have an effect.

they caught us halfway thru the third,
and from there the game became a contest of pure will to win.
the lead went back and forth,
neither team leading by more than 2.
the volume in the gym was deafening.
we were struggling on offense,
they had made excellent defensive adjustments.
but their shooting had cooled considerably.
i don't think anyone had made them run and work as hard as we
were.
tired shooters are not as accurate,
and our defensive adjustments were working out as well.

then, in the 4th quarter, the team we had scouted showed up.
a couple of stops on their part,
a couple of missed shots on ours.
a few great offensive moves on their end.
suddenly we were down by 7,
and had a must-score possession.

we got the ball inside;
their guards dived down, like they had been doing all night,
and knocked the ball loose.

we kicked it out of bounds,
and suddenly we were staring defeat in the face.
3 minutes to go, down 7, and they had the ball.

our pregame plan had us scoring a lot in the paint.
we thought we saw holes we could exploit.
but your opponent wants to win as much as you do.
they had anticipated our plan,
and their diving guards had given our inside players fits all night.

coach mike called time out;
"ok, men. this is it. we're going red."
our guys looked grim. everyone could taste defeat.
they also looked determined.
looking around at their faces, while mike ran down assignments
the whole season flashed thru my mind.
the little team that wasn't supposed to win at all.
the little team that refused to lose.
i could see in those intent faces...

this thing wasn't over yet.
it was hopeless.
but it wasn't over.

the official called us back to the floor.
there was time for one closing instruction.
"guys. you just have to get the job done."
sometimes in sports there is no secret.
you just have to get the job done.

they weren't exactly surprised to see a press.
(there was no other choice in our position, either try to press
or give up and lose)
but, at least we had no presses on tape for them to have studied.
their guys would have to figure it out during play.
i was grateful for the timeouts we had forced them to use in the
first half.
they would not have the luxury of simply getting a good look at
our press,

then calling timeout so their coach could tell them how to dissect
it.
(and we did have 2 versions, that looked the same, but attacked the
ball different)

the press is a funny thing.
it can be devastating, but the press is inherently weak.
any time you put two men on the ball,
someone is not covered at all.
you have to press with about 10 times normal defensive intensity.
if you let people think, and look at the floor,
the press will do nothing but give up easy baskets.
so the first key is to find yet another gear.
i knew our guys were going to be dragging something out from
deep inside themselves.
something they might have never known was there.
the only other choice was to lose.
the odds were great that we would lose anyway.

our crowd had been silenced before the timeout,
but they had not given up on us.
their fans were ecstatic.
the total pandemonium in the gym, as the teams come back on the
floor, was invaluable to us.
i don't think coaches or players either one were really aware of the
crowd any more.
but their coach would not be able to shout instructions to his
players.

another key to our press is what we let their players see,
during that brief moment they have to get rid of the ball, before the
pressure closes.
our object is not to take away every outlet.
we want him to see a man open.
we just don't want him to have time to see the player rotating over
to steal the pass.
the open man has to be behind the guy coming to trap.
every basketball player that ever played knows,
that his outlet is most likely going to be where the trap is coming

from.
from elementary school on, that is where they are taught to look
first.
we could not allow him time for a second look.

they brought it in,
they made 2 careful passes across the backcourt,
studying how we were set up.
trying to figure out what we were going to do.
they could not play that game forever,
there are only 10 seconds allowed to cross midcourt.
they made up their mind and tried to go.
the next pass, we exploded into action.
they had guessed wrong.
turnover.
score.
we switched versions of the press
turnover.
another score.
we switched back.
incredibly, a third turnover.
we scored again.

their coach called timeout.
he still had a 1 point lead, and the ball.
there was 2:07 left, and we were back in the game.
we were still in a hole.
they still had the lead;
and the ball.
but even their veteran team had to be a little rattled.

we knew we couldn't press again.
that man on the bench had gotten a good look at us.
and now he had a chance to communicate with his guys.
if we pressed again, it would not be us scoring the quick basket.

we had only one advantage.
both teams were nearly out of timeouts.
we were using his to go over how to defend their version of 20.

we knew they'd be running it,
and we had seen it live.
he was using his to explain how to beat a press they would never
see again.
when you are the underdog, it pays to have the other guy
responding to you,
instead of making you respond to him...

always take the white pieces!

after running quickly thru the assignments,
coach mike added;
"if it gets down to 40 seconds, we have to foul; not you, blake"
(blake already had 4 fouls and we could not afford to lose him)
blake said;
"we aren't going to have to foul."
will finished his thought;
"they can't hold it on us for 2 minutes."

the look on their faces said that was not an idle boast.
they absolutely believed it.

i remembered blake, back in elementary school.
he was a funny looking little guy on the floor.
always so serious about his play.
but he was a winner.
he worked like a mule,
and he always played his best in the biggest games.
he has grown older and bigger.
but he has not changed a bit.

will was our only player who had not been with us since
elementary school.
after his 6th grade year,
his school's basketball coach did not take him on their middle
school team.
told will that he was too small and too slow to ever be a basketball
player.
(that school is already preparing for next year)

his parents let him transfer to our school in the 7th grade.
we have a place for anyone who truly wants to play ball.

i remember the first time i saw him.
he was too small and too slow.
still is...

what a hell of a basketball player he has become.
when the game is on the line, we want the ball in his hands.

at the end of this game,
one locker room was going to be full of tears.
the other with cheers.
if our road ended here, some of the tears would be mine.

as i feared; they ran their delay well,
and we could not catch up.
all the delay games are basically the same.
spread out the floor,
keep the ball moving and away from the defense.
when they are forced to foul, hit your free throws.

our opponents were deadly shooters.
and we could not catch up with the ball.
the seconds ticked away.
we needed a miracle.
and then we got it.

we couldn't catch the ball,
but we could stay close enough to prevent them from relaxing.
their best player got a pass, and started to pass the ball on...
blake anticipated the pass and jumped into the passing lane.
their guy didn't throw the ball away,
but that awkward moment had committed him to moving,
and he could not get the ball down in a dribble fast enough...

walk.

our ball!

we called timeout to set up the play to take the lead.
our next to last timeout.
we would have to save the other until the very end.
games have been lost for the lack of one timeout!

we didn't get to run the last play.
one of their guys gambled on a steal, and gambled wrong.
he fouled will.
the foul put will on the line for a 1-1.

the first hit nothing but net.
tie score.
the second was a mirror image.
we were ahead.

1:17 left, and they used their next to last timeout
to set up the go ahead play.
we knew he'd be saving his final TO until the last seconds, as well.

the game was going to be decided by his seniors,
who do not want it all to end,
against ours.

i don't talk in the huddle that much.
better to run things thru mike, and let one voice give instructions.
time is too short for confusion.
this time,
when he finished his defensive instructions,
and said
"anything else?"
i spoke up;
"20?"

"yes. if we get it back with the lead, go 20."

our defense held.
it wasn't perfect, they got off a decent shot.
but we had pressure on the shot, and it clanked off.

we rebounded and came down the floor;
me and mike screaming "20!!!" "20!!!!"
if one player forgets, it can cost you the game.
a one point lead is not much to run 20 with,
but we have faith in our guys.

they had to foul, and it was will again.
he sank both ends of the 1-1,
and we were up by 3.

they came down and scored to cut it to one,
then it was will's turn to calmly sink 2 more free throws.

it went a couple more possessions,
them fouling will as soon as he got the inbounds pass.
will hitting every free throw,
with the season on the line on every one.
them hitting an answering basket with the same pressure.
but always 2 pointers.
we were arrayed to defend the 3-point line,
and would not let them get off a shot to tie.

it finally got down to 13 seconds,
and they used their last timeout.
this was it. they could not score another 2.
it was a 3-pointer or nothing.

we anticipated their play perfectly,
and there was no shot possible.
they made a couple of extra passes,
desperately searching for an opening.
we scrambled, and covered them up.

as the clock neared zero,
they had no choice,
one of their shooters flung up a prayer.
not really even a shot,
just a 2-handed sideways fling.
as the time slipped off the clock,

i watched it arc towards the basket.
it was eerily reminiscent of that godawfulnightmare that cost us the
thompson's station game.
except this one was on target.
no wild ricochet off the backboard,
it hit inside the rim....

made a half circuit and rimmed out.
one of their guys rebounded it as the horn sounded.

all of a sudden, i could hear the crowd.
i mean REALLY hear the crowd.
our people were going nuts.
our players were running across the floor,
laughing and crying and hugging each other.

we had been so beaten.
and then we won.

it couldn't last long.
we had to do the handshake line.
i am proud of our guys.
we were respectful.
i felt so bad, watching the line of sad faces go past.
they were a good team.
they won so many games
and they went so far.
they were neither laughing, nor crying.
the tears would start in the locker room.
when their coach gave that hardest post-game talk of all.
the one that says;
"that's all guys. it is over...

there is no tomorrow."

it had to be even harder tonight.
when they saw our tapes, they were sure they would win.
when they saw us warming up, they knew they would win.
and when we called time out with 3 minutes left, they HAD won.

playing ball can bring the greatest joy.
but, for every team save one, the season ends with tears.

our post-game talk was short.
we have much left to do.
it ended with;
"two more games to state!!"

will asked me the big question.
back at the start of the season, after our disastrous first game,
talking about where we had been picked...

dead last, not winning a game,

i had told the team i would shave my "whole head" if we made it
to state.
i have done my part.
my playoff beard and what passes for hair have been untouched.
(i am no carl, but am definitely getting the homeless look)

the guys wanted to know,
"when (WHEN?) we win that second game, do we get to have a
piece, or are you just going to go home and shave?"

"well, right now there is no second game. we only have one more
game on our schedule.
But, if you earn that second game, i will bring a scissors."

i pulled up a handful of beard;

"i think there is enough here for everyone to take a hunk."

it was worthy of a cheer.

it was a great night.
good enough to savor for a little while.

i saw their coach heading out.

he looked so sad.
i know the feeling.
anyone who has really coached knows the feeling.
losing is always tough.
losing a game that you had won,
that is the worst.
losing it in the tournament...

proper etiquette said i should speak first (i think)
"y'all played a great game tonight."
"thanks, you have a really good team."
"y'all are just as good. it is hard when the game is this close."
"yes.... it is really hard... good luck to y'all"
"thanks."

another time and place, i could have wished him good luck, as well.
but he had no more tomorrows.

i went home and started thinking about our next opponent, trace creek.
celebrating time was over.
we scouted them last week, as well.
they are huge. they are fast. and they are really, really good.
they are 27-2, and one of the favorites in the state.

not a favorite to get there,
but a favorite to win there
(except for when they draw AHA, of course; AHA has
already made a space in their trophy case, and sized their
championship rings)

we have 2 days to get ready.
there is a lot of work to do.
i reckon we will be big time underdogs.
there isn't anyone left in the tournament that looks anything like us.
but that won't be anything new for our guys.

i checked before i left the gym.
they set the scoreboard back to zeroes.
i reckon tomorrow will be whatever we make it.
so far we have made a 20-3 out of our tomorrows.

we want 21 really bad.

the last practice

once again,
i prepare to go to what might well be our last practice.
you never know for sure when your last practice will be.
so it is like approaching execution dates,
with a series of last minute reprieves.

this time of year,
the period between one game and the next is packed.
against ever more challenging opponents,
you have a limited time to formulate a game plan,
and convert that to something you can get across in a single
practice.

the opponents are brand new,
not the familiar faces you have come to know during the long
season.
there is a good chance,
you might have never seen them in person,
and all you have is film.

film can never replace being there.
there are nuances to a team that cannot be captured on film.

seeing a team can never replace having played them.
actually tasting something yourself
is not the same as smelling it cooking,
and watching someone else taste it.

i was at case's yesterday,
and had the luxury of watching film on his good internet.
i admit, i wasted too much time watching the burrito play.
but you don't get another season of baby.

i saw her perform a new feat, for the first time,
and shake her hand in the air,
suffused with the joy of victory.

her face, during her victory dance, reminded me of our guys
and the celebration after the miracle comeback the night before.

the process of game planning is a unique thing.
i watched the film with almost a sense of foreboding.
trace creek is a team of many strengths,
and few weaknesses.
i was trying to find anything we could exploit.
any facet of the game that we could be the better team.
the object of any game plan,
is to make the game play out in ways that favor your own team.
you want to find the key to controlling the game,
deciding how it will be played,
ideally, bending your opponent to your will.

the list of things we could not afford to let them do was long.
the list of chinks in their armor seemed nonexistent...

at first.

you start out with a handful of "what ifs"
getting a feel for their habits, and preferences;
and wondering how to take them away from what they find most
comfortable.

lucky for me, the final decisions belong to coach mike.
i did not have to create a whole game plan,
just come up with contributions.
i knew coach mike was spending his evening the same way
(except for the burrito distraction)
down by normandy, old coach charlie was undoubtedly doing the
same thing.
coach charlie has been an extra resource all season long,
studying film and crafting strategies.
coach mike is not one to let his ego get in the way of using every
resource at his disposal...

sometimes even I make a contribution.

at first, it was like there was nothing there.
it was like watching a preview of our own execution.
but trace creek is not AHA.
they haven't been able to scour the country for players.
they are a high school basketball team,
and they are not perfect.
as i ponder, i start to see a few things.
not big things.
this guy doesn't go left.
this guy doesn't do well guarding small, quick players.
you can tell when they are going to do this...

after a while, it is like blowing up small slices of a big picture.
those vulnerabilities fill the screen.
and i start to ask myself;
how can we use that to our advantage?
what can we do that will focus pressure on the weak point?

e-mail has changed the world.
by that night i was able to e-mail coach mike my thoughts.
my observations and early concepts for global strategy.

his answer confirmed my suspicion that he is a genius.
most of our ideas and observations dovetailed.
i was sure that coach charlie was already represented in there.

coach mike is a great collaborator.
a lot of coaches have difficulty incorporating other people's ideas
into their game plan.
they follow their own sole voice,
even when everyone else is telling them they are making a mistake.
(when everyone thinks you are wrong, you have to be an idiot not
to entertain some doubts)

i know who i am.
coaches mike and charlie know more x's and o's than i will ever
dream about.
i am the "quality control" coach.
i see the game from a perspective that only a long-time 6th grade

coach can see.
and sometimes i see things from that perspective that have value.
when i see things in the game plan that i know are mine,
it gives me great pleasure and pride.
but i know not to forget who i am.

subsequent communications start drilling down to tactics.
a tweak to a defense.
moving someone around on offense.
altering our rotation and switching up some player groupings.

by the time we are closing in on practice time,
there is a whole picture in my head of us winning;
and exactly how we are going to do it.
the hopeless images that flittered across my screen yesterday are
gone.
coach mike is busy converting all that into a practice plan.
one that enables us to prepare the guys for what they need to do,
in just an hour and a half.
you cannot accomplish more by simply throwing time at the
problem.
there is a limit to how long practice is effective.
by the end of practice,
we want the guys leaving with the same images in their heads,
that we have constructed in ours.
if practice runs too long,
you stop learning and start losing ground.
it is a good thing we have been in the planning together.
the kids will hear a single message.

i left out the self-scouting.
under normal circumstances you also scout yourself.
you ask yourself;
"what would i do, if i was him?"
anticipating the other guy's game plan can be a major victory.
in this case, self-scouting is easy.
they are bigger, stronger, and faster.
they have better shooters, better ballhandlers, and superior
defensive play.

their game plan is to come out and do what they do best...

and make us like it.

their coach would have to be an idiot to put in something special,
just for us.
they are 27-2. pretty good indication that he is not an idiot.

when the two teams take the floor tomorrow,
there won't be more than 15-20 people who honestly believe we
can win.

as long as they are all on our bench,
that will be as many as we need.

well, time to head for practice has come.
i'll let you know how it goes.

strategy and tactics

it was a long ride to the tournament site.
a pensive ride.
i told sandra i had no real expectation of winning tonight.
she wasn't shocked.
she still thinks i should expect to win every night,
no matter what.
i think you have to be realistic.

then i told her that if the guys could pull off our game plan.
we might just win anyway.

i felt really good about our game plan.

the strategy was pretty simple.
trace creek is big, fast, strong, and talented.
they like to play in runs,
going up and down the floor like it is a tennis match,
rocking their opponent,
and just burying them.
we intended to make them play a possession by possession game.
looking at how they had won,
they had won a lot of games in the first quarter.
the first quarter was critical.
we didn't expect to win it.
we didn't really even want to.
they had been challenged by people early before.
they came back and rolled them up like rugs.
we just wanted to be there at the end of the quarter.

if trace creek had something i saw as a weakness,
they only play 5 people.
we would be playing 8.
it could have been 9, but one guy missed practice yesterday.
if you haven't gone over the game plan,
you won't be much use in the game.
we would be fresher in the closing stages.

we just had to keep the game competitive until then.

of course, a strategy is nothing,
if you don't have tactics to implement it.
you know that when your opponent is this good,
you can't take away everything.
sometimes your policy has to be to give them what they don't
really want.

one key player, after watching a while,
we realized that all his scoring came off moves to the right.
like any one way player,
his best moves all started with a feint to the left.
his defender had to be planted directly in the path to the right,
and had to stay there no matter what.
it wasn't that their guy couldn't go right.
he didn't want to.
during yesterday's practice,
i went from player to player that would be defending him,
during their time on the sidelines from the group work,
and went over their positioning defending this man, individually.
they nodded, agreed, and repeated back to me what they were
supposed to do.
one thing that makes our players better than their physical talent.
they are good at carrying out assignments.

another player had an oddity in his game.
his dominant hand was not the one he shot with.
on film, we had just thought he was remarkably proficient at using
his off-hand
(he had a devastating dribble drive)
but he was betrayed by his own people,
by a casual (and seemingly innocuous) comment on his
handedness.

armed with that knowledge, we switched up our approach.
we would make him go to his shooting hand all night.
it was not that he could not do it.
he was good with either hand.

but using your non-dominant hand requires greater concentration,
greater mental effort,
than using your strong hand.
it makes you more tired, because the brain is a fuel hog.
we were going to make him think that his favorite hand had been
amputated.
by the end of the game,
he would be a lot less effective.

another player was a demon on the offensive boards.
at times, his put backs constituted a huge percentage of their
offense.
his defender's only job on defensive rebounding was to eliminate
him from the play.
our guy might or might not get a single rebound to his credit,
but he was the key to our defensive rebounding.

people who read the stat sheet, and think they know who made
plays,
don't really understand the game.

on down the list, our defensive plan was a collection of
assignments.
we didn't expect to shut these guys down.
we just wanted to dictate what they did.
we tailored the assignments to our guys' individual abilities.
some of the matchups might look crazy to the people in the
bleachers.
but we felt pretty good about what we had cobbled together.

our offensive plan was a throwback.
me and coach mike both go back to the days before the 3-point
shot.
since the advent of the 3-point shot,
one of the most important weapons in the game of basketball has
come to be almost abandoned.
the mid-range jumper is nearly extinct.
players are admonished against shooting a 15 footer, when a shot
from 3 feet further is worth an extra point.

offenses have come to consist of inside shots and long bombs.
defenses have mirrored the change.

our guys work on the mid-range jumper every day.
we value it, and it is an integral part of our offense.
to put it simply, a 15 foot shot that you hit is worth 2 more points
than a 20 footer you miss.

these guys have played a 2-3 defense all year.
nothing else.
they are so long, and so tall and so fast,
that opponents wanting to shoot 3's are forced out to 25 feet or
more
(and then it is hard to get a good look)
their big post was a dominating defender.
he just made other team's big guys disappear.
there was no way to get the ball to them.

looking at the film, we could see trace creek simply suffocate other
team's offenses.
but when we took out eyes off that,
we saw something else...

big spaces.

most of the time, basketball talk is about gaps;
seams in the defense to drive thru.
they were so much quicker than us, that there weren't very many
gaps to exploit.
but they defended so large an area,
that they left huge spaces inside the defense.

if we could spread out our offense,
and get them to match it with the defense...

then slip people into those spaces from the offside.

we had lots of good things available.
mid-range jumpers.

or attack the basket with the dribble.

our guys pass the ball well on the interior.
we might have a huge disadvantage with one of our posts against
theirs.
but a guard and a post combining to attack the basket changes
everything.

and they only play 5 guys.
when we get an advantage, they have to protect their fouls.

our leakers into the spaces were to be like body punches.
if we caused enough pain to the midsection,
eventually the hands had to come down.

then we would get our 3-pointers.

it was a good plan.
but there was one component more important than all the others.
compete.
we had to compete for every second of the game.
we had to stay in it in the first quarter.
and let the cumulative effect wear them down over the next two.
we only wanted to win one quarter.
the 4th.
we aren't much to look at.
but, by god, we compete.

i did not come into the gym with an expectation of winning.
there was no justifiable reason to think we could win.
but my mind works in compartments.
and the realistic compartment shut off for the day when i walked in
the door.
we were here to win a ball game.
by the time warmups started, the gym was already packed.
the tournament was at a new school,
and the gym was the biggest we have ever played in.
our fans filled a whole side.
i saw people i haven't seen in years.

there is nothing like a tournament run in a small-town.

their side was just as full.
they have been a powerhouse for a long time.
but this was one of their special teams.
we were but a minor hurdle on the way to the state.
they expected to cheer for another rout.
our scroungy band of runts would be easy pickings,
a breather on the tough tournament road.

i liked the look of the warmups.
they were casual, relaxed and happy.
joking and cutting up.
our game films are a potent weapon.
watching us play,
it is easy to forget that we are winning those games.

the pre-game talk was encouraging.
we were the most focused i have seen us all year.
the guys were about to jump out of their skins.
tipoff couldn't come soon enough.

the opening quarter was right out of our script.
they came out swinging,
looking for the quick knockout.
we scrambled, scratched, and clawed, to stay in the game.

twice they opened up 10 point leads,
and we seemed to be on the ropes.
each time we found a way to string together some baskets
and make some stops
and fight our way back in the game.

we were down 6 or 7 going into the second quarter.
right where we wanted to be.

they shared one weapon with us.
they loved to make the long downcourt pass for quick scores.
it had done a lot of damage for them in every game we saw (live or

on tape)
i felt good about our ability to defend that.
we practice against it every day.
by the end of the night, we would not give up a single basket on a
snowbird.
we would ring up two.
both huge.
Even bigger than those critical points…
both teams had to sprint downcourt on every possession.
they only had 5 guys to do it the whole game. we had 8.
and most of our players had a fall of cross country interval work
under their belts.
it was a scoring draw, but a strategic advantage for us.

you know, i almost never actually notice the crowd during a game.
but, while we were fighting for our lives in the first quarter,
every time there was a lull in the sound,
some jerk a row or two behind our bench could be heard loudly
criticizing the coaching.
at one point, during a timeout,
he proclaimed that;
"if we had coaches, we would be ahead by 10, instead of behind by
10."
not that it was important,
i have scouted enough games to know that there are blowhards like
that in every crowd.
i just wondered why he thought he should sit right behind our
bench.

it didn't matter for long.
by the middle of the second quarter the crowd was so loud
we had to speak right in their ear to talk to the person next to us.
we had turned the game into the game we wanted.
possession by possession,
every one was life and death.
they had punched themselves out, looking for the early KO.
we rolled out fresh bodies, and slowly the aggressor changed.
point by point we chipped away at their lead,
and their crowd who had been raising the roof exhorting them to

blow us away
were even more desperately screaming for them to hold us off.
our crowd, who had come out of the excitement to even see us in
this game,
was going berserk to see us actually competing.

the last couple of minutes was all us.
we actually had the last possession, down by 1, with a chance to
take a halftime lead.
but we were unable to get off a shot.
if i had written up the game i had dreamed about, before it
happened,
this was how it would read.

it was an easy halftime.
we ran down a few breakdowns in our assignments.
we made a few minor adjustments.
and then we went back out.

i would have loved to be a fly on the wall in their dressing room.
they had not been in this position very often.
at 28-2, and only having lost to AAA teams,
they had been having their way with AA competition all year.
and now they had their backs against the wall with a team that
looked like it belonged in single A?
"who are those guys??"

we have been here before.
been there all season.
we knew we had to weather the storm.
all we wanted was a game that came down to the final minutes.
at 28-2, they had not been in that situation that often.
we have spent our season in that situation.
and our guys may not be the greatest at many things.
but they win close games.

they made their run.
but there were no 10 point leads,
no threats to run away with the game.

our attacks on inner space were starting to take a real toll.
every time they pulled out to a small lead,
we answered with a series of short jumpers,
or 2 on 1 under the basket.

as the third quarter wound down,
it was trace creek up 2 , with the ball.
they were playing for the last shot.
in a game this tight,
being up 2, 4, or 5 going into the final quarter
as opposed to being tied or behind…
that was huge.
a smart team takes the last shot at around 5 seconds.
that way there is no chance of the other team getting off a shot.
trace creek took theirs at 7.
if you recall, after a rebound we can be shooting a layup in 3.5
seconds.
we recall it.
we run that drill regularly.
the guys can run it in their sleep.
and we know to keep running after every rebound…

especially late.
that is when people are tired
that is when they can lose focus.
jesse pulled down the rebound on the baseline,
and waverly relaxed.
there were only 4 seconds left,
only enough time for jesse to dribble out around halfcourt and fling
up a prayer.

 But jesse didn't dribble.
he fired a pass out to hayden, on a dead run near halfcourt.
hayden didn't miss a beat,
he wheeled, and fired a pass to the basket.
austin was there to take the pass in stride and lay it in.
the horn sounded as the ball nestled into the net.
it was countless drills paying off

it was our season in a nutshell.

i heard the crowd this time.

moments into the 4th quarter we took our first lead.
it did not seem possible, but our crowd found a few extra decibels.
their crowd matched it.

after the pummeling beneath the ribs in the third,
the hands finally came down.
they started collapsing their perimeter defense to stop it.

just like we had pictured it watching the film,
we ripped them with uncontested 3-pointers.

at one point we opened the lead to 7.

but good teams do not go down easy.
season on the line, they came screaming back.

there is nothing quite like the final minutes of a game like this.
the stakes are everything or nothing.
and the winner could be either team.
there is no way to describe the clarity and focus.
coach mike ran our team like a finely tuned instrument,
the players responded with exactly what was asked.
it was like i knew what was coming up next in my responsibilities,
before it even happened.
i can't describe the feeling.
man must have been made to be a part of a team.
the joy of playing your own role,
being a part of something bigger.
at that moment the team was functioning like a single organism.

oh, but they were not finished.
our opponent had been wounded,
but they were far from dead.
they got within 1 several times.
each time our guys refused to let the lead get away.

as the game went from 1 to 3 to 1 to 3,
the roar of the crowd went back and forth across the gym.
looking back, i wonder if anyone in the gym was in their seats.

with a couple of minutes left,
we finally got the stop that allowed us to run 20.

this was no bunch of newbs,
that let precious time run off the clock while their coach tried to be
heard over the noise.
they immediately fouled.
they remembered the game films.
we might not be impressive at much,
but our 20 has been rock solid.
they knew we would not be turning the ball over.

they had reached a point in the game,
where they were going to score on every possession...

by sheer force of will if they had to.

our guys were going to have to hit the most pressure packed free
throws of their lives.

for a couple of possessions the score went from 5 to 3.

then they hit the jackpot.
about 30 seconds left and they fouled a man who missed the front
end of a 1-1.
it took them about 4 seconds to cut our lead to 1.
another quick foul, and will sunk 2 more to push it back to 3.
i wondered to myself,
how many clutch, end of game free throws in a row did that make
for will?
i didn't have time to come up with an answer.
getting in big guys on defense, and free throw shooters on offense
was my job.

with 9.8 seconds left,

will was shooting free throws to get it back to 3.
the game was now in the final act.
they could not afford another 2,
they had to tie.
they used their final timeout.

our time out instructions were simple.
and cruel.
we force them to throw it in short,
and make them dribble upcourt to burn some seconds.

as soon as they crossed midcourt,
we were to foul.
they would get free throws....

TWO free throws.

will fouled their ballhandler at midcourt with 4.6 seconds left.
fans are fans.
ours were crying out in outrage;
"that was no foul! are you blind ref? whose side are you on?"

time and score, people, you have to understand time and score.

they hit both, to cut the lead to 1,
and we had the ball in to will so fast it would make your head spin.
we knew, if they had a chance, they would make sure he could not
get it.

ideally, he could have dribbled most of the remaining time off the
clock.
but this team was just as smart and experienced as us.
they landed a crushing foul on will with 4.2 seconds to go.

it took him a long time to get up.
we pleaded uselessly for an intentional foul
(which would have given us the ball back)
it should have been one.
but officials are loathe to make calls that decide games.

so will had to shoot clutch free throws one last time.
as he came up the court, he was limping.
one side of his face was red,
and it looked like he had the beginnings of a black eye.
i thought, for a moment, that his nose was bleeding.
but it was just running from being smashed.
they would have probably allowed us to replace him from the
bench...

but who would we rather have in this situation than will?

he calmly sank the first, to make it a 2 point game again.

i leaned over to coach holly and shouted in her ear;
"we might be better off if he misses this one. they won't be able to
get much of a shot."

i was wrong.
he missed,
they got the rebound out, fast as lightning.
3.5 seconds,
remember that time?

it takes 3.5 seconds to take a rebound and get it to the other end for
a layup.
we had enough presence of mind to prevent that.
but it is also enough time to get the ball in position for a 3-point
attempt.

they got it there.
it was a hurried shot,
but it was a pretty good look at the basket.

once again, the horn sounded as we watched the ball arc towards
the basket.
if it goes in, we lose.
(how many times does this make?)
it was like all the sound, and all the air,

sucked out of the gym,
as every person in the building watched the ball track thru the sky.
half praying for it to go in.
half praying for it to miss.
and everyone with 20-100 vision or better could see it was going to
be close.

it was a good shot.
they have great shooters.
but it was not a perfect shot.
it came down inside the cylinder and caught just enough rim to
rattle back and forth over the opening...

and roll off.

suddenly i could hear the crowd again.
everyone was screaming.
our players were running and jumping and hugging,
laughing and crying.

this is the furthest that our school has ever gone.

we had to sober up quick.
we had a handshake line, with yet another stunned opponent.
a worthy, talented, capable opponent,
who had just lost a game they thought they could not lose.
i felt sympathy that i had no way to express.
but our guys were respectful.

in the locker room, it was again insanity.
the guys told me i better have my scissors ready.

there is a meaningless seeding game with AHA tomorrow.
they looked almost bored, winning their game with ease.
irritated, actually, that their opponent persisted in playing to the
very end.
their crowd was small, and seemed disappointed that they didn't
get as many highlight reel plays as usual.
they don't usually turn out that much until the state finals.

this is a long trip to make on a weekday;
for a game you cannot lose.
it doesn't seem like it would be that much fun.

monday is the day.
we will play another one of the best teams in the state.
the other seeding game is between two teams expected to contend
for number 2.

monday we play for real.
we either go home, or we go to state.
i have a lot of film to watch...

and i need to locate a pair of safety scissors.

realistically, we have no chance to win.
we are too small, too slow, and not athletic enough to match up.
but i don't trust these guys around my head with pointed scissors.
we don't know where we will play yet,
but i have it on good authority,
the scoreboard will start at zero to zero...

and tomorrow will be what we make it.

underdogs part 25

we got a good look at what is in front of us monday.

here is a surprise.
they are a lot bigger than us.
(they had a number of impressive dunks tonight)
they are faster than us.
they are 12 deep.
and i think their fans are already reserving motel rooms at state.

it was a great game between teams ranked 3rd and 6th in the state in AA.
(and they were ranked there for good reason)
they played balls to the wall for 32 minutes,
the previously undefeated team losing when the tying shot was off target at the horn.

there could not have been higher stakes.
the winner gets to host us monday.
(our recent string of success has boosted our overall ranking to 95th!)

the loser has to go and get put out (painfully) by AHA.

personally, i think we should be ranked a little higher,
since there are only 48 teams left playing.
but i have seen us on film, so i understand.
a lot of better teams than us have already gone home.

we got to see everything they had.
they are a great team, no doubt about it.
but they are a high school team.
they are not perfect.
now we have 3 days to try to patch together some sort of game plan.
something that will just keep us in the game until the end.
we really should have picked an easier path thru the tournaments.

this will be our 5th game against a team in the top 10.

realistically, i do not expect to win.
only a fool would bet on us to stay within 20.
and yet, it was a great trip home.
me and coach mike talked about what we saw
(i tell you, he is a genius; we saw the same things)
we talked about what we are going to do in practice tomorrow,
about what we have to do in the game.
i don't know how to explain it,
but there is something about a great challenge that makes the light
brighter,
and the air sweeter.
it makes the blood course in your veins.
it makes you more alive.

so monday night we will find out.
one more game.
we need one more miracle.
this isn't the movies.
this is real life.
and in real life you don't always come out on top.
but these guys have been thru so much this year.
and no matter what has happened, they have never flinched.
never given up.
they were written off before the first game was ever played.
and they have been written off at every step of the journey...

but they are still here.
and they still intend to go to the state.

what else can happen

what else can happen to these guys?

today's game was not going to be the biggest game of the year.
not to say that it isn't the biggest game of the year.
but it is bigger than that.
this was supposed to be the biggest game in the history of the
school.

during the 30 some odd years since the orange has existed,
exactly 4 basketball teams have reached the substate.
none have won that final game to reach the state.

to be fair,
during most of those years,
the orange has been one of the smallest schools in the state.
we did not have sport specific athletes,
almost all the boys had to play,
just for us to have teams.
i remember football teams with 14-16 players,
and one year when they were down to 11,
and dressed out the manager so they could keep 11 on the field
when someone was shook up.

when i started coaching the 6th grade team,
most of the boys in the 6th grade played.
otherwise we couldn't field a team.

the new century has brought a lot of "growth" in our area.
the last couple of years, we were finally a good sized class A
school.
and our sports teams became a lot more competitive.

during my years as 6th grade coach,
i had 3 special teams.
teams that had the potential of one day reaching the state.

the first team ended up just missing the substate.

the second bunch never won like they had as 6th graders.

the third special team was this year's seniors.
they didn't exactly knock your socks off when they walked on the
floor.
they are too small.
too slow.
just a pretty mediocre looking bunch of kids.
if they came into a restaurant where you were eating,
you might never guess that this was a basketball team...

all they have done is won games.

but it has seemed like everything was stacked against them.
their first 3 years of high school,
they played for 3 different head coaches,
with 3 completely different systems.

last year, we found out they would get screwed during
reclassification.
even tho there are a larger schools than us playing in class A,
a technicality in the classification rules for football
got them bumped up to AA...

in one of the best top to bottom AA districts in the state, year in
and year out.

they made the most of their last year in class A,
notching a great regular season record.
but then, in one of the few letdowns this bunch has ever had,
they stumbled in the first game of the tournaments.
this team that had looked like the best shot the orange has ever had
to make state,
went home after the first game.

this year looked grim.
if our new district wasn't a tough enough row to hoe as it was,

AHA got tossed in there to boot.
why AHA plays in AA is beyond my comprehension.
but there they were.
we have two teams in our district who have no business playing in
AA.
at the furthest ends of the scale.

after a 30 point shellacking in the first game of the season,
these guys had every reason to be discouraged.
we had been picked to finish dead last.
we were not expected to win a single game as an AA team.

instead, they told me that they were going to the state.
i felt sorry for them.
they were going to be ridiculously outmanned every night.

you guys know the rest of the story.
here we sit, 21-3 against high school teams,
only one win away from going to the state.
we got hit with an outbreak of mono late in the season.
the healthy guys promised the sick ones that we would still be
playing when they got back.
somehow, missing players i thought we could not get by without,
we kept winning.
this has been one of the miracle seasons i have ever witnessed.

the last few games in the tournament have been astounding.
the deeper we get, the more out of place we look.
our greatest weapon has been the difficulty that other coaches must
have,
convincing their team that we have to be taken seriously.
we have had to put together game plans with baling wire and duct
tape.
playing teams where we are outmanned at every position,
this special group of young men has not looked impressive.
they have just won games.

with AHA matched up with us from the very beginning,
we have had to win, and win, and win,

so that we only meet them in each championship round,
and don't get eliminated by the automatic loss.
then we have to fight our way out of the bottom bracket in every
tournament,
playing all higher seeds,
just to take another thrashing in the finals.
we have yet to be able to claim our rightful 1st place in anything.
but here we are, one game from the state.

our guys have not been the least discouraged.
after the first experience with AHA (a 61 point loss)
we simply did the math, and worked out the brackets.
then we set our goal at playing them 5 times.

we are up to 4.
if we can make it to a 5th, it will be at the state.

but first we have a substate game to get past.
the team we are facing is ridiculously more athletic than us.
we still have our one advantage.
reading the HS basketball chat site, where the substate games are
now THE hot topic,
a total of one person included the word "if" in front of "eastland
beats the orange."
they have a "mr basketball" type player.
our top player came to us in the 7th grade,
because he was considered too small and too slow to play class A
basketball.

we have our gameplan.
and we have had a couple of the most intense practices i have ever
been a part of.
when we left the gym yesterday,
i knew we were as ready to play as any team can ever be.
i was so pumped that i stayed up until 0300.
and woke up at 0500.
ready to roll.
even for me, 2 hours is a pretty short night.
but we are playing in the biggest game in school history.

it was supposed to rain last night, followed by a little sleet.
they got 5 inches of ice on the ground north of us.
and tonight's game has been moved to tomorrow night.
what else can happen?

i have put off surgery on my mouth for an uncomfortable month,
scheduling it for the beginning of the gap between substate and
state...

tomorrow.

tomorrow afternoon they put me under and do surgery on my
mouth.
i have been working out rides all day,
to get me to the game.
(no way i can drive)
i have responsibilities to my team during the game,
and there is no substitute to fill in for me.
we don't let each other down.
i might be a small cog in the mechanism,
but once in a while i make a contribution.

the best laid plans

if trace creek had been one of the most challenging game planning
opponents,
eastland was one of the easiest.
trace creek presented so many different threats,
and had so many ways to beat you,
that initially the task seemed impossible.
great long range shooting, a powerful inside game.
trace creek was a tough nut to crack.
but here we were, and trace creek had gone home.

we scouted eastland live, when they were knocking off previously
undefeated ashland.
(as expected, ashland fell to AHA in their substate by 30 some
odd points)

we watched tapes.
the eastland formula for success was consistent.
they had the shooting, they played nasty tough defense,
challenging everything.
they cut off passing lanes, stealing every pass that was too long, or
too weak.
except for their mr basketball contender, they were a cookie cutter
team.
a long bench of tall, lean, athletic, greyhound types.
mr basketball was cut from the same mold, but from a much bigger
piece of material.

like so many of the athletic teams we had been facing,
they came out like a house fire, and tried to blow people away right
out of the blocks.

but the backbone of their game was offensive rebounding.
they were relentless,
coming in waves.
other than a couple of critical players, they simply rolled in fresh
bodies in a never-ending stream.

fouls and fatigue were immaterial.

in the ashland game, eastland had flown at the boards from all directions.
during the first quarter, they had second, third, even fourth chances to score.
they just kept getting the ball back until they got it in the hole.
ashland had come out in the second half with a new commitment to boxing out,
and it had almost, but not quite, been enough to take back the game.

trace creek had beaten eastland during the season, by taking away the second chances.

of course, trace creek and ashland had something we did not have.
they had size, and athletes to match up.

none the less, we saw the task as definable.
and, if it is definable, it is doable.
that was the message to the team;
"we CAN do this."

we knew eastland would be able to shoot over us.
they shot over the much taller players from ashland and trace creek.
but they did not run multiple complex offenses.
they either ran a 5-out motion offense...
frequently clearing out one side for their greyhounds to take the ball to the hole,
or, if they got a size advantage,
they put mr basketball in the post and fed him the ball.

we understood they would be able to score on us.
a lot.
but we also knew we would have opportunities to get runouts and snowbirds...

if we could only get rebounds!

and we felt like our multiple offenses would have some success
against their gambling defensive style.
but we would also be one and done.
with their speed, we could not sell out for offensive rebounds.
we had to be getting back, or the snowbirds would be living on our
end of the floor.

the whole game hinged on us holding them to one shot per
possession.

the biggest question we faced was what to do on defense.
the best way to box out is to play man defense.
that way, everyone has a man they are responsible to box out.
and the only way we were going to get any rebounds was for every
man to box out his man first,
and get the ball second.
if we tried to chase rebounds we would be jumping at air.
we would look like little kids playing keep-away with grownups,
as all the rebounds would be taken away above our heads.

it is infinitely harder to box out from a zone.
finding the man to box out, before he already has the rebound is
problematic.

me and coach mike discussed the problem.
if we played a man defense,
we weren't sure that any of our guys could stop any of theirs on the
clearouts.
we couldn't play the standard 2-3,
because we were too small and slow to extend it over their range.
and it might be impossible to box out from it.
our various trapping zones were out,
because the other team has to have someone we can trap.

almost by default, we were going to have to try and use the
matchup zone.
to be honest, that defense is best suited to messing up the passing
lanes.

and while eastland could run some passing sets that left you
looking foolish,
it was their "outside shot as an insertion pass" that scared the heck
out of us.
the matchup gave us a zone's hope of stopping penetration,
and altho the assigned man changes as the offense rotates,
we would have some semblance of boxout assignments.
coach mike ran some intense zone-box-out drills in our last
practice.

our secret weapon seemed to be lost.
all season long, the media love affair with AHA had been a great
help to us.
every day (even the days they did not play)
the headlines in the high school basketball coverage was AHA.
the teams we were beating were lost among the anonymous
box scores.
the only time people saw our name, we were getting beat by 40, 50
or 60 points.
that is a convenient way for your opponents to envision you.
we had too many quality wins for that to work for us any more.

on the way to the game, it felt someone had driven tenpenny nails
into my mouth;
luckily, the guy who worked on me played ball.
before he put me under,
he told me that when i woke up i should go home.
take my pain pills.
"and sleep for about 24 hours."
i told him i was coaching in a substate game in a few hours...

"after the game;
go home, take your pain pills and sleep for about 24 hours."
i like him. he gets it.

i also had little realistic expectation of winning.
but my ride got me there just in time to see the team going in the
door to the gym.
i ran to join in the end of the line,

so i did not have to mumble my way thru the pass gate.
soon all the insignificant stuff;
like us not having a chance, or my mouth hurting, faded into the
background.
it was game time.

during warmups it was obvious that our disguise had been
penetrated.
eastland was all business,
none of the joking and kidding around that had preceded many of
our most stunning victories.
we were being judged by the string of scalps on our belt,
not by our unimposing physical appearance.

eastland came out blazing.
our matchup zone was powerless.
no defense is effective against a team that is hitting everything they
put up.

on offense, we were just as powerless,
their high pressure man to man thwarting every attempt to run
anything.
almost before we knew what was happening,
we were down 13-2.
we knew they would hit the court looking for a quick knockout.
it was nothing we had not experienced before.
and no team hits every shot forever.

we had not gotten this far on our physical prowess,
but it was not like we had no weapons of our own.
versatility was our strength.
we could run a lot of offenses and defenses.
so far we had been able to find a weakness in every high school
team we had played.

there is a saying, that every battle plan lasts only until the first shot
is fired.
and it is a nearly universal truth.
trace creek had been a true miracle...

the flawless game plan.
against eastland, we had to improvise under fire.
we had been right about the runouts.
eastland crashed the boards so hard, that we could get the
snowbirds...

when we got rebounds.
we had been totally wrong about the matchup zone on every count.
it scarcely slowed the powerful eastland offense.
and we were completely unable to box out and rebound from it.
there was no choice but to go man.

after a quarter, we trailed 28-13.
early in the second quarter, the deficit climbed into the 20's.
it is only natural to lose a little edge when the opponent seems
beaten.
our guys were reeling,
but surrender is not a part of their makeup.
as ferocious as the eastland assault had been,
these guys had seen much worse.
the AH beat them by more than 60,
but they got back up and went willingly to play them again, and
again.
they wanted nothing more than to play them once more.
you could knock these guys down.
but they were gonna get back up.

we managed to battle our way back within 18 by halftime.
it was a daunting deficit.
but not insurmountable.

at the half we solidified our first half adjustments.
we had come into the game expecting our inside game to be
neutralized.
eastland had almost completely eliminated the inside game of
much bigger opponents.
but the eastland game plan had been to eliminate our outside threat.
we switched the second half focus to attacking the bigger team

inside.
we abandoned all hopes of using zone defense.
we had to get some rebounds.

of course, we were sacrificing a lot of our ability to stop their
offense.
that could not be helped.
even at the risk of giving up runouts
(which were all going to end up in monster dunks)
we had to commit more resources to crashing our offensive boards.
we had to outscore them.

the goal was to cut the deficit to 10 or less by the end of the third.
that would give us a chance in the 4th.

it might have sounded crazy.
but it worked.
we caught them off guard when we came out blazing in the second
half.
we were supposed to be cowed and beaten.
we didn't just whittle away at the lead,
over the first 4 minutes we cut the lead to 7.
our crowd, which had been silenced during the brutal first half,
gradually came to life,
gaining enthusiasm with each point we closed.

eastland came back with a flourish.
they could score in bunches,
while we had to will each score to happen.
their lead exploded back to 15,
and then we chopped away at it.
there would be no rout.
our guys were not going to allow it.
10 points at the end of the third. that was the goal.
and we ended up winding the clock down with a 13 point deficit,
looking for the one last shot to put victory within reach.

we ran it perfectly, setting up the one good shot,
and draining it with just a couple of seconds on the clock.

it was a huge momentum play...

destroyed when they threw a quick pass to midcourt,
and nailed a 40 foot buzzer beater to put us back down by 13.
it had been that kind of a night.

underdogs.
we had been the underdogs all year.

it was no longer a question of coaching or strategy and tactics.
the last 8 minutes was purely about the will to win.

we came back and cut the lead to 7 once more,
before they put on another run.
god, they could score so fast.

we would not go away.
both crowds were getting their money's worth in the second half.
there were going to be a lot of croaking "tournament throats"
tomorrow.
but, by now the clock was our enemy.
we made one last push.
with less than 2 minutes left, we got it down to 7 one more time.
then we got the stop, and had the ball.
if we could only score once more,
the pressure would all be on them.
no one has won more games in the last 2 minutes than our little
band of giant killers.
up until this possession, i had been too busy to think about winning
or losing on an emotional level.
but at this point i became merely a spectator.
it was all in the hands of the guys on the floor.
we had to have a score.
in a season filled with miracles, could we possibly have one more?

great moments are what define the great players.
good players make lots of plays and score lots of points.
great players make the plays when the season is on the line.

it was not a bad pass.
it was not too long. it was not lazy, or careless.
but mr basketball showed why he is mr basketball.
(besides the 37 points he torched us for)
with almost supernatural anticipation, and the quickness of a cat,
he cleanly stole a 5 foot pass at full speed.
he almost seemed to materialize in the passing lane.
had he guessed wrong,
one of our best shooters would have been left with an uncontested
3.
had he mis-timed his jump, he would have sent us to the line for 2
free throws
(and we hit 17 of 17 free throws on the night)
but neither of those things happened.
instead mr basketball raced down the floor unchallenged for a
backbreaking dunk.

actually, it ignited a run of 3 consecutive turnovers,
all followed by dunks,
that put us back into a double digit deficit.

oh, we played the intentional foul game.
we hit some shots, and sent them to the line hoping for some
misses.
we even got it back under 10, one last time.
but, when they hit a pair of free throws to go back up 11 with 15
seconds left,
it was time to make sure the last 5 players on our bench got to go
on the floor in a substate game.
they have worked all year, just like everyone else.
and not many teams get to play in a substate game.
this might be the only chance they ever have.

we stayed in the locker room for a long time.
there were a lot of tears.
not over a lost game.
we had done everything we could do.
but, over the end of an era.
these young men had been like a part of my family from the time

they were little boys,
learning to shoot left handed layups correctly.
they had done thousands of drills.
we had sat together on the bench for hundreds of games.
we had been through crushing losses and glorious victories.
there was a love in that dank room,
smelling of sweat and leather and liniment,
that only those who have been in a hundred dank, smelly locker
rooms can understand.
no one wanted it all to end.
i remembered, for the first time in a couple of hours, that my
mouth hurt really bad,
and i wanted, make that needed, to lay down and go to sleep.
but i didn't want it to end either.
when we walked out of that locker room, it would be into a
different world.
maybe will might get to play somewhere for a few more years.
the rest of them will be young men moving on into the real world.
no more practices, no more games, except just for fun.
these boys that i had watched grow up, would walk out of my life
forever.
when next we met,
if we meet again on some future day,
we would greet each other with joy,
and talk of the great times we had.

and i know they will ask the half question, half statement they all
ask;
"we were really good. weren't we?"
"yes. you were. you were really good."
and we will smile a secret smile.
that passes between men who have walked on the floor with giants,
and walked off, more often than not, with a new skin for their wall.

a song runs through my head, every year,
when the seniors walk out of the locker room for the last time.
i can't remember the name of the song. or all the words.
just the sad refrain;
"i hope you had the time of your life"

in a couple of weeks it will be time to start preparing for the next
season.
this year's juniors will be seniors next year.
soon to realize how short their time has become.
there will be new challenges.
more giants to face.
and i will tell sandra;
"most people my age have given this up.
i don't know if i have what it takes to get thru another year...

maybe it is time for me to retire."

and she will answer;
"and do what? sit at home and wait to die?"

soon afterwards i will be yelling at kids running drills;
"use your left hand! we are going to keep doing this until you do it
right.
and then we are going to do it a thousand more times.
we don't know who will go to state next year, but we know this
much.
they are doing drills right now. and they are doing them the right
way."

The End

Made in the USA
Lexington, KY
28 November 2018